hot for food

VEGAN COMFORT CLASSICS

hot for food

vegan comfort classics

101 RECIPES TO FEED YOUR FACE

LAUREN TOYOTA

TEN SPEED PRESS

California | New York

contents

hey hot for food fam!

Can you believe you're holding my first cookbook?
I can barely believe it either.

For those of you new to the hot for food fam, I'm Lauren Toyota and I created hot for food a number of years ago just for fun. I didn't understand blogging, I was skeptical about the YouTube platform, and I wasn't even vegan when it all began! But now here I am with a cookbook full of hot vegan recipes and a YouTube channel with devout obsessive foodies following along every week, and I'm totally happier living this vegan life!

The original blog entries and awful WordPress template from the first incarnation of hotforfoodblog.com circa 2010 are long gone, thank god! But the passion I have for vegan food hasn't changed and has only gotten bigger since then.

After nearly a decade hosting television, I took a leap and decided to make hot for food my career in 2014. At the time I was dating John Diemer and together we were cooking up all kinds of vegan love! He was curious as to how we could make all of his favorite meaty, cheesy meals with plants, and before long he was hooked on the lifestyle. That sparked a new vision of what hot for food could be—something fun, real, and comforting. We had all these ideas on how to grow the brand and get more people making vegan food (that wasn't boring). That's where producing videos came into play, and we launched a YouTube channel. Prior to 2015 we had never picked up a DSLR camera. I learned how to take pretty good food photos, and he started playing around with the video settings. One day we just made a recipe video, and the rest is history!

Making a cookbook wasn't something I had on my bucket list, honestly. Circa 2015 I even claimed in one of my YouTube Q&As that I probably, most definitely, would not ever make a hot for food cookbook. Well aren't I embarrassed! But I gotta give it up to the universe for throwing this opportunity my way. It knew something I didn't. I needed to make this cookbook, not just for me, but for you! It was something y'all kept asking me about and I could never let you down. Thanks for the nudge—I'm so thrilled to share this book with you.

What you've got in your paws is a shiny printed version of some of hot for food's most popular recipes and more than eighty more brand spankin' new ideas that will not appear anywhere else. The photos are all new too. My resistance to creating all this was just a big ol' bunch of fear, and believe me, that fear kept rearing its ugly head during the entire process of birthing this thing. But great challenge brings even greater reward. I guess the task of creating a book was so much more pressure for me than delivering YouTube videos every week. Prior to this career path I spent nearly a decade hosting and producing television, so I'm comfortable being on camera and editing video, but I certainly hadn't wrapped my head around publishing a book. A book is permanent, it lives on forever, and I can never go back and edit something. I'm also asking people to pay for it. I've been fortunate enough to give you all the recipes and content for free up until now! So I think that all got to my nerves. A few panic attacks and lots of hours of meditation later, it all came together. This truly has been one of the most rewarding, eye-opening, and biggest learning experiences of my life. For that I'm beyond grateful!

why hot for food?

I honestly don't remember when, why, or how I came up with the name hot for food. But I feel like it's how I've always felt. You too, I bet!

My entire day revolves around food! During breakfast I'm thinking about dinner. During dinner I'm thinking about what I'm going to make on the weekend. The only way to find solace is to manifest these thoughts as delicious recipes! If John and I are taking a trip, it most definitely focuses around trying to stuff as many restaurant adventures as we can into whatever time we've got. Once we almost missed a flight home from Hawaii because we went hunting for vegan chicken wings in Waikiki! Ummm, totally worth it! They're at Downbeat Diner & Lounge by the way.

why vegan?

Because I can't stomach food any other way! But it took me a long time to realize this. I spent my teenage years as a vegetarian and my college years in a constant dilemma over whether I should go back to being vegetarian or not. Bottom line: I just felt sick and guilty every time I ate meat, dairy, or eggs, but my love of food and stubborn attitude about not wanting to be a bother at the dinner table kept me stuck to old habits. Finally, in 2009 I couldn't take the stomach pains and emergency bathroom breaks any longer. I had also just watched the documentary *Food Inc.* and that led me down a path of ferocious learning. That research helped me decide once and for all that I needed to go vegan. I started blogging my transition on hotforfoodblog.com, and by January 1, 2010, I would no longer eat animals or animal by-products. My only regret is not doing it sooner!

Also eating animals is just weird to me. We're socially conditioned to do it and have done so throughout history. But we don't have to do it, especially in this day and age.

I've always had a strong love for animals, and something always resonated deep inside me that didn't feel right when I ate meat. Plus now the issue of what to eat is so much bigger and more confusing than any of us can even grasp. Do I really need to tell you that animal agriculture is the leading cause of climate change? Our food choices matter, and whether you eat vegan all the time or most of the time, or even just occasionally, it's a step in a good direction for all of us on Earth. So that's that.

feed your face

I want you to devour this cookbook the same way you binge-watch your favorite shows: ferociously! My mission from the start has been to show the world how good vegan food is and how easy it is to indulge in all your favorite foods without feeling guilty.

I know a lot of rumors are going around that vegans can't eat deep-fried food, ice their cakes with sugary buttercream, or consume fat and salt. Who would want to hang out with someone like that? Not me. I'm of the belief that as long as it's free of animal-based ingredients it's A-OK to eat it! So that includes things like gooey cakes, fried everything, and salty snacks. My motto is maintain a balance of foods I should eat with foods I want to eat, and make these two things one in the same whenever possible.

Right now there are enough vegan cookbooks with healthful grain bowls, raw granola bars, and sugar-free cookies. We don't need another one. So it's time someone broke the rules! You want french fries for dinner? Duh! Who doesn't? And you should be able to eat them without judgment. Besides, if it's our recipe for Loaded Fries Supreme (page 140) with The Nacho Cheese (page 205) made from carrots and potatoes . . . well that's practically a salad anyway!

Needless to say, this book isn't meant to be a meal-planning guide or an example of how to eat a balanced vegan diet. You can find that kind of stuff with a Google search. Within these pages are recipes for indulgent, delectable, gourmet vegan comfort foods that you crave. Foods that the majority think someone who's vegan couldn't eat. So to all the omnivores out there . . . anything you can eat, I can eat better AND vegan. I'm in the business of making food porn. Tasty, drool-worthy vegan creations that mimic the flavors, textures, and feeling of dishes traditionally made with animal-based ingredients. Your other vegan books are just a tease; this is the real deal.

the recipes

Whether you want to take your vegan diet to places you never thought were possible or you're an omnivore looking to broaden your horizons in the kitchen, this book is totally worth devouring. I aim to inspire you to cook, love eating, and feel great while doing it. Check out the collection of Badass Brunches (page 7), Oodles of Noodles (page 113), and Finger Foods (page 33) to get the ball rolling. Then graduate to The Main Event (page 137) and Sweet Things (page 167) to impress your family and friends. For simple, easy meals and sides, turn to Hearty Soups (page 70), Stacked Sandwiches (page 90), and Veggie Sides & Big Salads (page 55). There you go . . . every dish you need to love going vegan (or vegan-ish) and an arsenal of recipes that'll convince vegan naysayers that plant based IS the future of food.

The pictures alone will have you panting, but there are also detailed instructions for every recipe plus some visual step-by-steps for some of the more labor-intensive creations I want you to master. Read every word and be on the lookout for *hot tips* with simple ideas on transforming meals or recipe components into new things. That way you can reimagine this food again and again and nothing goes to waste! You'll start to love and appreciate leftovers like never before.

When it comes to deep frying, just call me queen. JK! But I seriously know how to deep fry like a boss and it's something I used to be terrified of too! You'll notice a few deep-fried dishes in this book and you need not be afraid. I recently invested in a deep fryer, which keeps things a little less messy, but it's totally not necessary. All you need is a wide heavy-bottomed pot and a clip-on thermometer to monitor the right temperature range noted in the recipes. Use a neutral vegetable oil like sunflower or canola and as long as your oil is hot enough then the water in the food will boil, evaporate, and prevent oil from seeping in and sogging up your food. When you do this enough you'll notice nearly the same amount of oil you put in the pot will be left afterward, so you're not ingesting a vat of oil! And yes, you can reuse it about six times. You need to cool it completely, then strain it into a glass jar or empty container. You'll always need about two inches of oil in the frying vessel unless you're using a deep fryer—then it often requires more. This is why I've noted a range or approximately the amount of oil required for frying the recipes. It will vary slightly depending on the vessel. In the case of a shallow fry, you'll use a lot less oil and you can use a cast-iron skillet or heavy flat-bottomed pan, as is the case with the Spicy Black Bean Taquitos (page 50) or Cripsy Crabless Cakes (page 53). These are more delicate morsels, so placing them flat into less oil to fry them and flipping them half way through will ensure a perfect result and nothing should fall apart. After a couple times you'll get the hang of deep frying and then you might get obsessed with it and have visions of opening your own food truck!

A reminder: These recipes have been tested only the way you see them written. If you're used to substituting ingredients and are familiar with the way other flours, oils, sugars, etc., perform, then go ahead and do your thing...but I can't promise perfect results. That's just how a cookbook works. There are many, many ways to make the same thing, but since these are my recipes I've made them the way I like food to taste with ingredients I like using.

what you need

Part of cooking well and having fun while doing it is having all the right kitchen tools on hand. It's taken me two years to accumulate pretty much everything I need, but it makes my life way less frustrating. Here's a list of the basic equipment beyond pots and pans that you'll need to use for recipes in this book.

- An **OVEN THERMOMETER** is a small device you put in your oven to show you the exact temperature. MOST ovens are not the temperature they say they are, and a thermometer can save you a lot of frustration.

- A **DEEP-FRYING THERMOMETER** is imperative for deep frying like a pro! I specify frying temperatures and ranges, so you'll need this tool. Guessing what's going on with hot oil is dangerous territory!

- A **SLOTTED FRYING SPOON** will help remove fried stuff with ease and will allow excess oil to drip off before removing the item from the pot.

- A **PASTRY BLENDER** is the best way to blend dough for a flaky pie crust.

- A **HIGH-POWERED BLENDER** is my true love. SOMETIMES a regular blender can work too but no guarantees!

- A **FOOD PROCESSOR** is my other love, but SOMETIMES you can do the same thing by hand.

- A **HAND MIXER WITH BEATERS** is a cheap and useful investment that will come in handy for making whipped cream and beating butter for baking. SOME people have fancy stand mixers. Good for you!

- **AN IMMERSION BLENDER** isn't necessary but is very handy for blending up soup directly in the pot and for making quick vegan mayo. It's also fairly inexpensive.

- A **WAFFLE IRON** is fun, but you only need it if you want to make waffles really bad!

- **PARCHMENT PAPER** is my go-to for ensuring things don't stick while baking, but it also helps crisp up certain things (like breaded cauliflower) where I find silicone mats don't. Plus paper looks good in food styling and photography, which is why I always have it on hand.

- **WIRE BAKING RACKS** are really handy for properly cooling your baked goods and deep-fried stuff.

- **SPATULAS** (of various sizes) are so handy! They help mix doughs, cake batters, and lift delicate baked goods. Use them to scrape every last drop out of pots, bowls, and your blender. Spoons are for fools! Heat-resistant silicone ones are my spatula of choice.

badass brunches

If you ain't about that brunch life, don't even talk to me! Brunch is the best meal ever invented. There's a whole ritual and culture built around it, something that's lacking from the everyday breakfast, lunch, dinner routine. Brunch is like the bad boy your parents never wanted you to date. He plays by his own rules and probably rides a motorcycle. Like Ryan Gosling in pretty much every movie, and you're the one who can't decide what you want to eat! Despite never being able to decide what I want to eat at brunch, I also like it because it's a little more indulgent, and then you can lounge around all day reminiscing about the rendezvous. Savor your weekends and treat yo'self with these recipes!

but first...bacon

Starting a vegan cookbook with a spread dedicated to plant-based bacon . . . that's my style. But seriously, the foodie obsession with actual bacon is annoying. There, I said it. Get with the times.

The future of bacon is before you . . . a tangy, sweet, and smoky marinade to drown endless options in. Then you can bake or fry up a ton of "baconlike" crispy stuff for any dish you're craving. These recipes make decent-size batches so you'll have leftovers and in many cases enough for multiple recipes in the book. The marinade below is the base ingredient, followed by some of my favorite options.

bacon marinade

¼ cup low-sodium tamari or soy sauce

2 tablespoons maple syrup

1 tablespoon liquid smoke

1 teaspoon smoked paprika

Combine all of the marinade ingredients together in a bowl or wide dish with a whisk or fork.

coconut bacon

3 cups large flaked unsweetened coconut

Bacon Marinade (see above)

Preheat the oven to 350°F.

Stir the flakes into the marinade and coat well. There shouldn't be any marinade pooling at the bottom of the bowl, as the flakes will soak it up.

Line a baking sheet with parchment paper. Spread out the coconut flakes in an even layer.

Bake for 20 to 25 minutes, tossing every 5 minutes to prevent burning. When the coconut is a uniform, deep brown color, remove the baking sheet from the oven and transfer the bacon to a plate or another baking sheet so it doesn't continue to cook. Allow it to cool completely before storing in an airtight container. The bacon will last 2 months if stored in a cool, dry place, but it never lasts that long in my house.

almond bacon

3 cups sliced, blanched almonds

Bacon Marinade (page 9)

Preheat the oven to 350°F.

Stir the almond slices into the marinade and coat well.

Line a baking sheet with parchment paper. Scoop out the almonds from marinade with a slotted spoon and spread in an even layer on the baking sheet. Reserve the excess marinade for brushing during bake time.

Bake for 25 to 35 minutes, tossing every 10 to 15 minutes to prevent burning. Watch closely as your oven temperature and bake times may vary. If the almonds are not darkening, you can brush on extra marinade halfway through baking. When the almonds are crispy, dark brown, and slightly sticky, remove the baking sheet from the oven and place on a wire rack to cool. The almonds may stick together, but once they're cooled and dry you can break them up with a sharp knife and store in an airtight container. The bacon will last 2 months if stored in a cool, dry place, but it never lasts that long in my house.

tofu bacon crumbles or slices

1 (about 14 oz/390 g) brick firm or extra-firm tofu (about 2 cups crumbled or sliced thin)

Bacon Marinade (page 9)

Preheat the oven to 425°F.

Depending on the use for the tofu bacon, either crumble it into small pieces or thinly slice it along the short side. Marinate the tofu for 15 minutes.

Line a baking sheet with parchment paper and either spread the crumbles in an even layer or lay out the slices spaced slightly apart. The tofu crumbles will have absorbed most of the marinade. For the slices you can reserve any excess marinade to brush on halfway through the bake time.

Bake for 25 to 30 minutes, flipping the tofu halfway through the bake time and brushing the slices on both sides with excess marinade. The tofu should be much darker when it's done. It might not be crispy right out of the oven, but it will get firmer as it cools.

Store in an airtight container in the fridge, and use immediately for a recipe or consume within 10 days.

mushroom bacon

1 tablespoon vegetable oil

Bacon Marinade (page 9)

4 ounces shiitake mushroom caps (about 6 large caps), sliced thin, or 2 large portobello mushrooms, sliced thin

Preheat the oven to 350°F.

Add the vegetable oil to the marinade and combine well.

Marinate the mushrooms for 15 minutes.

Line a baking sheet with parchment paper. Lay out the mushroom slices spaced slightly apart from each other. Reserve the excess marinade for brushing during bake time.

Bake for 25 to 30 minutes, flipping the slices and brushing with excess marinade halfway through the bake time. At the halfway mark, you may notice that any smaller pieces of shiitake mushrooms are already pretty crisp. Remove these pieces and place aside until the remainder is finished.

When the bacon is crisp and slightly sticky, remove from the oven and transfer to a plate or another sheet to cool completely. Store in an airtight container in the fridge, and either use immediately for a recipe or consume within 7 days.

cassava bacon

1 cassava root
Bacon Marinade (page 9)
1 to 2 tablespoons vegetable oil, for frying

Peel the tough brown waxy skin from the cassava and discard. Your cassava root should be firm and white, not gray or mushy. That is a sign of spoilage.

Using the peeler or a mandolin, shave off thin strips of cassava about 1¼ inches wide to resemble strip bacon.

Marinate the strips for 15 minutes.

Heat a nonstick pan over medium-low heat with a small amount of oil. When the pan is hot, place 4 or 5 strips into the pan. Cook for 3 to 4 minutes on the first side and 2 to 3 minutes after flipped. You may need to lower the heat so the pan doesn't get too hot and burn the bacon. Once or twice while frying a batch, add a little bit of the excess marinade to help caramelize the bacon. Also add more oil to the pan before frying each batch.

Remove the fried strips from the pan and set on a plate. Placing the strips on paper towels isn't advised, as they will stick.

The bacon lasts up to 2 weeks stored in an airtight container at room temperature or in the fridge. Warm up leftover strips in the oven or in a pan on the stove before serving with recipes.

the big brekky skillet

MAKES 4 to 6 servings
PREP TIME 35 minutes
COOK TIME 45 minutes

prep ahead

Coconut Bacon (page 9)

potato hash

2 pounds baby white potatoes, quartered (about 8 cups)

2 tablespoons vegetable oil

1 teaspoon paprika

1 teaspoon sea salt

½ teaspoon ground pepper

2 garlic cloves, minced

tofu scramble

1 (about 16 oz/450 g) brick medium-firm tofu, crumbled

1 tablespoon vegetable oil

2 shallots, minced

2 green onions, white and green parts, finely chopped

1 cup finely chopped red bell pepper (about 1 pepper)

2 tablespoons nutritional yeast

1 teaspoon ground turmeric

½ to 1 teaspoon sea salt

¼ teaspoon ground pepper

¼ cup unsweetened nondairy milk (optional)

toppings

½ cup packed, stemmed, and finely chopped kale leaves

½ cup vegan cheese shreds (optional)

1 avocado, pitted, peeled, and sliced

½ cup Coconut Bacon

1 tablespoon finely chopped chives

Hot sauce

This is my go-to breakfast option every weekend. It's perfect for serving a household of hungry mouths, though John and I have been known to devour the whole thing between us! Serving meals in a skillet makes me feel warm and fuzzy inside, and somehow even makes the meal taste better.

Preheat the oven to 450°F.

To make the potato hash, place the quartered potatoes in a pot of cold water and bring to a boil. Cook until fork-tender, approximately 8 minutes. Drain and set aside.

Meanwhile, prepare the tofu scramble. Drain the tofu and pat dry of excess moisture with a tea towel or paper towel. Heat a large cast-iron skillet or oven-safe pan over medium heat and add the vegetable oil. Add the crumbled tofu, shallots, green onions, and red pepper and sauté for 3 to 4 minutes or until the vegetables are softened and about half cooked.

Add the nutritional yeast, the turmeric, up to 1 teaspoon of the salt (adjust to your taste), and the pepper. Stir to combine and cook for another 2 minutes. At this point you can add up to ¼ cup of the nondairy milk if the mixture looks too dry and cook for another minute. Remove the scramble from the pan to another dish and set aside.

To cook the potato hash, wipe out any excess scramble from the skillet and heat over medium heat. Add the vegetable oil, potatoes, paprika, salt, and pepper and toss to coat the potatoes well.

Cook for 12 to 14 minutes, stirring only a couple of times and allowing the potato quarters to crisp on the bottom. Add the garlic and cook for 2 more minutes, lowering the heat slightly to prevent burning.

Add the scramble on top of the potatoes in the skillet or transfer to an oven-safe casserole dish if you can't put your pan in the oven. Surround the scramble with the chopped kale and top with the cheese shreds.

Bake for approximately 15 minutes or until the kale looks crisp and the cheese is completely melted and slightly browned.

Top with the avocado slices, bacon, and chives before serving. Add hot sauce to taste to individual servings if desired.

flaky buttermilk biscuits

MAKES 10 biscuits
PREP TIME 30 minutes
COOK TIME 10 minutes

ingredients

1 cup unsweetened soy
or almond milk

1 tablespoon apple cider vinegar

2 teaspoons freshly squeezed
lemon juice

2 cups all-purpose flour

2 teaspoons baking powder

1 teaspoon baking soda

½ teaspoon sea salt, or
1½ teaspoons sea salt if using
coconut oil

5 tablespoons cold vegan butter
or cold solid coconut oil

Jam and vegan butter,
for serving

These are going to go faster than the free biscuits at Red Lobster . . . my favorite childhood restaurant. I wanted to leave them as a blank canvas so you could experiment with additions, but if you want to make them cheesy (like the ones from said restaurant), just add 2 tablespoons each of nutritional yeast and freshly chopped chives, then add as much vegan cheddar shreds as you can handle. Hollaaaa! And if you're going for a fancy dinner roll, then fold in fresh herbs like rosemary or thyme, some ground pepper, and call it a night.

Preheat the oven to 450°F.

Combine the milk with the vinegar and lemon juice in a small bowl. Set aside for 10 minutes to curdle.

In a large bowl, combine the flour, baking powder, baking soda, and salt with a whisk or fork. (If you're making cheesy biscuits, add the nutritional yeast here.)

Cut the cold butter or oil into the flour mixture using a pastry blender until you have a crumblike texture.

Create a well in the middle of the dry ingredients and pour the liquid mixture into it. (If you're adding any other extras, do it now.) Then gently fold the batter a few times until just combined. Do not overmix!

Lightly grease a baking sheet or line with parchment paper.

Place the dough on a floured work surface. Lightly flour your hands and gently flatten the dough until it's approximately 8 to 10 inches wide and 1½ inches thick.

Lightly flour a 2 to 2½-inch round cookie cutter and cut out as many biscuits as you can. Place the biscuits on the baking sheet.

Try not to handle the dough too much, but create another, smaller round of dough with the same thickness as before and cut out more biscuits until only a scrap of dough remains.

To get extra lift in your biscuits, lightly poke a fork a few times across the top of each biscuit. Bake for 10 minutes and serve slightly warm with jam or more vegan butter.

the best breakfast sandwich

MAKES 5 sandwiches
PREP TIME 20 minutes
COOK TIME 25 minutes

prep ahead

Cassava Bacon or the bacon of your choice (page 11)

vegan egg

1 (16 oz/450 g) brick medium-firm tofu

¾ cup unsweetened nondairy milk

⅓ cup nutritional yeast

¼ cup tapioca flour

1 teaspoon ground turmeric

1 teaspoon garlic powder

1 teaspoon onion powder

1 teaspoon sea salt

½ teaspoon ground pepper

2 tablespoons finely chopped chives

3 tablespoons vegan butter, for frying

sandwich

5 English muffins, split in half

5 tablespoons vegan butter

5 vegan cheddar cheese slices

Cassava Bacon

2 vine tomatoes, sliced thick

Now I know y'all get excited about fast-food breakfast sandwiches but the speedy prep always makes them look so lame! That, and they often lack quality ingredients, which makes them a total gut bomb. But now all your dreams are alive and they're layered together in this dreamy breakfast sandwich. It's so seductive you'll forget why you ever ate eggs in the first place.

To make the vegan egg, drain the tofu of excess water. Place in a high-powered blender with the nondairy milk, nutritional yeast, tapioca flour, turmeric, garlic and onion powders, salt, and pepper. Blend on high until smooth. The batter should be the consistency of a thick pancake batter. Add a bit more nondairy milk if you need to thin it out. Stir in the chopped chives.

Heat a nonstick pan over medium heat and add a bit of vegan butter. Let it melt and spread it around the frying surface. Pour approximately ⅓ cup of the batter onto the pan and gently spread out to a 6- to 7-inch circle. Cook on the first side for 4 to 5 minutes; the patty should be bubbling and look slightly cooked through and darker in color before flipping. Flip and cook for another 4 to 5 minutes. Fold the patty in half and then in half again, so it looks like you've folded a thick crepe, and cook for another minute on each side to make sure that the middle is thoroughly cooked. Set each folded patty aside on a plate and cover to keep warm. Butter the pan before pouring the next ⅓ cup of batter into the pan. As you go, you might need to lower the heat or adjust cook times, as the pan will get hotter.

When you're on your last egg patty, set the oven to broil and place the English muffins on a baking sheet. Generously butter each side of the muffins and place 1 piece of cheese on each of the bottom halves. Toast under the broiler for a couple of minutes until the cheese is melted and the muffins are golden brown. Watch closely so the muffins don't burn!

Place the bacon strips in the pan once the egg patties are done just to heat through.

To assemble each sandwich, place an egg patty on top of the cheese, add a tomato slice and as many bacon strips as you want, and finish with the top half of the muffin. The patties can be made ahead and heated through in a pan or the oven or in a microwave before serving. You can also store extra batter in the fridge for up to 4 days.

hot tip If you're a real badass, skip the English muffins and put all this stuff on the Flaky Buttermilk Biscuits (page 15). Next level!

baked bean tostadas

MAKES 6 tostadas
PREP TIME 25 minutes
COOK TIME 30 minutes

prep ahead

The Sour Cream (page 210)

baked beans

2 tablespoons vegetable oil

½ cup finely chopped onion
(about half an onion)

1 teaspoon smoked paprika

1 teaspoon mustard powder

1 teaspoon sea salt

½ teaspoon ground pepper

3 cups cooked navy beans,
or 2 cans (each 15 oz/425 g)
navy beans, rinsed and drained

1 cup water

⅓ cup packed brown sugar

¼ cup maple syrup

1 tablespoon apple cider vinegar

1 tablespoon tomato paste

1 teaspoon vegan
Worcestershire

collard greens

1 tablespoon vegan butter
or vegetable oil

10 cups packed, stemmed, and
finely chopped collard greens

3 garlic cloves, minced

½ teaspoon chili powder

¼ teaspoon sea salt

¼ teaspoon ground pepper

tostadas

12 corn or flour tortillas

2 teaspoons vegetable oil,
for frying

The Sour Cream

¼ cup finely chopped red onion

When I was growing up, canned baked beans were a thing in my house. My dad was obsessed. He still drives across the border to get a brand we can't find in Canada! So I had to come up with a recipe that matches the taste he's come to love. Besides, as an adult I've never ventured down the aisle to buy these things because they're laced with corn syrup and pork. No thanks! A homemade version has been a long time coming, and you can go ahead and eat these on their own or with toast, but I thought they deserved an inspired breakfast tostada to let 'em really shine!

To make the baked beans, heat the vegetable oil in a saucepan over medium heat and sauté the onion for 3 minutes until just softened. Add the paprika, mustard powder, salt, and pepper and cook for another minute.

Add the beans and the water and stir to combine. Add the remaining baked bean ingredients and bring to a simmer. Cook for 20 minutes, stirring occasionally. You can cook the beans for slightly less or more time depending on how much liquid you like in your beans.

Meanwhile, to make the collard greens, melt the butter in a large cast-iron skillet or nonstick pan over medium heat. Sauté the greens with the garlic, chili powder, salt, and pepper for about 10 minutes until soft, wilted, and dark green in color.

Remove the collards from the pan and keep covered to stay warm while you crisp up the tortillas in the same pan. Lower the heat if the pan is too hot. Fry the tortillas in small batches in a bit of vegetable oil for 2 to 3 minutes each side until golden brown and crispy.

Assemble the tostadas with 2 tortillas per tostada. Add the warm baked beans and collard greens, and top with the sour cream and chopped red onion.

Refrigerate any leftover baked beans for up to 4 days. You can also freeze the beans for longer storage. Thaw in the fridge overnight and heat through in a saucepan before serving.

tofu benny with hollandaise

MAKES 4 servings
PREP TIME 20 minutes
COOK TIME 20 minutes

prep ahead

The Hollandaise Sauce
(page 218)

tofu

1 (16 oz/450 g) brick medium-firm tofu

¼ teaspoon smoked paprika

¼ teaspoon sea salt

¼ teaspoon ground pepper

1 tablespoon vegetable oil

toppings

10 cups packed baby spinach or stemmed and chopped kale

Sea salt and ground pepper

2 vine tomatoes, sliced

The Hollandaise Sauce

4 English muffins, split in half

4 tablespoons vegan butter

Small handful of chives, for garnish

¼ teaspoon ground cayenne pepper, for garnish

This popular dish from the blog has saved my ass many times whether I'm hung over or entertaining the in-laws, so I knew it had to be included in this book. Though I was an eggs Benedict superfan back in the day, I haven't ever fantasized about the traditional version once since creating this masterpiece. Give tofu a real chance if you haven't yet. It comes in many textures, and all it requires is proper seasoning and cooking technique! If you thought your vegan life would never let you dive deep into a plate full of bennies again . . . you're welcome!

Drain the tofu and pat dry of excess moisture with a tea towel or paper towel. Slice the tofu into quarters and slice each quarter in half lengthwise, so you have 8 thick medallions.

Season the tofu on all sides with the paprika, salt, and pepper.

Heat a large cast-iron skillet or nonstick pan over medium-high heat and coat the bottom with a thin layer of vegetable oil. Place the pieces of tofu in the pan and fry for about 3 minutes on the first side. Flip and fry for another 3 minutes. The tofu should develop a nice golden crust. Continue turning the pieces to fry all sides.

Remove the tofu to a dish, cover to stay warm, and set aside.

Lower the heat to medium and sauté the spinach with a pinch each of salt and pepper until just wilted and cooked through. Remove the greens from the pan. Then fry up the tomato slices for 1 minute each side.

Warm up the hollandaise sauce and toast, and butter the English muffins.

Top each muffin half with greens, a tomato slice, a piece of tofu, and a dollop of warm hollandaise. Garnish with the chives and a sprinkle of ground cayenne pepper.

hot tip Here's another dish where you can skip the English muffins and go beyond with layering everything on Flaky Buttermilk Biscuits (page 15). Just sayin'!

mushroom & leek quiche

MAKES 6 to 8 servings
PREP TIME 1 hour
COOK TIME 55 minutes

prep ahead

The Parm (page 207)

The Red Pepper Relish (page 212)

pastry

2 cups all-purpose flour

1 tablespoon sugar

½ teaspoon sea salt

1 cup cold vegan butter, cubed

½ cup ice-cold water

filling

1 vegan chicken-flavored bouillon cube dissolved in 1 cup hot water, or 1 cup low-sodium vegetable stock

2 cups thinly sliced leeks

2 cups sliced cremini mushrooms (about 5 ounces)

1 cup diced asparagus (1-inch pieces)

1 tablespoon olive oil

1 shallot, finely chopped

1 garlic clove, minced

½ to 1 teaspoon sea salt

½ teaspoon ground pepper

1 tablespoon finely chopped sage

1 tablespoon finely chopped tarragon

1 (16 oz/450 g) brick medium-firm tofu

¼ cup nutritional yeast

⅓ cup chickpea flour

If I'm out to prove you don't need to eat eggs for breakfast, then I better re-create a dish that's essentially all eggs. You can customize this quiche to your liking by using substitutions for any of the veggies—try spinach, green bell pepper, or caramelized onions. Just be sure you cook the veg before adding it to the filling. The Red Pepper Relish (page 212) is what makes this quiche taste nostalgic for me though. My dad would always have chile relish at breakfast with our scrambled eggs, so it's the only thing I know, and it's essential!

To make the pastry, combine the flour, sugar, and salt in a large bowl. Cut in the cubed butter with a pastry blender until a crumblike texture is formed with small pea-size pieces of butter throughout. Create a well in the center of the mixture and pour in the water. I fill a cup with ice and water to ensure that the water is very cold. Just make sure you don't get ice cubes in the pastry. Fold the pastry together a few times with a spatula until just mixed but still crumbly. Do not overmix the pastry! (For step-by-step photos, see page 195).

Portion half of the pastry on a large piece of plastic wrap. Lift the sides of the plastic over the pastry to bring it together and gently form a ball. Finish wrapping the pastry in the plastic and gently flatten into a thick disk. Do the same with the other half. Refrigerate the pastry for at least 15 minutes before rolling out. You can also leave it up to 24 hours in the fridge, but it may need to sit at room temperature for 5 minutes to soften slightly before rolling out. You only need one portion for the quiche, so you can save the other half for another recipe, or roll it out as directed, place it in a pie pan, and freeze it for later. Bake the shell, without thawing, as directed below.

Have ready a 9-inch pie pan. Flour the work surface, your hands, and a rolling pin and roll out one portion of the pastry to a round ⅛ to 3/16 inch thick, stopping every couple of rolls to make sure the pastry isn't sticking. Gently lift the pastry and lightly flour underneath as you go.

The pastry should be at least 3 inches wider than your pie pan all around. Roll the pastry over the floured rolling pin, transfer it to the pie pan, and

CONTINUED

1 tablespoon white wine vinegar

1 tablespoon freshly squeezed lemon juice

1 tablespoon cornstarch

1 teaspoon mustard powder

½ teaspoon ground turmeric

½ teaspoon smoked paprika

Toppings

1 tablespoon The Parm

The Red Pepper Relish

roll it over the top of the pan. Gently press the pastry into the bottom and sides of the pan. Trim the excess evenly, leaving ¼ inch to work with around the edge. Fold the excess up onto the rim of the pan and gently pinch evenly all around the circumference to create a beveled edge. Prick the bottom and sides of the pastry with a fork. Freeze for 15 minutes.

Preheat the oven to 425°F.

Cut a square of parchment paper larger than the pie pan so it covers the sides. Fill about halfway to the top edge of the pan with pie weights or any kind of dried bean. Bake for 12 minutes. Remove the parchment paper and pie weights and bake another 2 to 3 minutes until the edges are just turning golden brown. Remove the crust from the oven, leaving it in the pie pan to cool on a wire rack. Turn the oven temperature down to 350°F.

While the crust is baking, make the filling. If using vegetable stock, you might need to add up to 1 teaspoon salt, as the bouillon tends to be saltier. In a large pan over medium heat, sauté the leeks (reserving 2 tablespoons for the topping), mushrooms, and asparagus in the olive oil for 3 minutes until the greens are brighter and about half cooked. Add the shallot, garlic, salt, and pepper, stir to combine, and cook for another 2 minutes.

Add the sage and tarragon and cook for another minute, then turn off the heat.

Drain the tofu and pat dry of excess moisture with a tea towel or paper towel. In a bowl, mash the tofu with a fork so it's well crumbled and combine with the remaining ingredients until all the tofu is well coated. Fold in the sautéed veggies and the stock and stir to combine well.

Spread the filling in an even layer in the pie crust. Top with the 2 tablespoons reserved sliced leeks and The Parm.

Bake for 40 minutes. The top should have a golden brown crust, and a toothpick inserted in the center should come out mostly clean.

Allow the quiche to cool for at least 20 minutes before slicing and serving. It should be warm but not piping hot. Top servings with the relish. Refrigerate any leftovers for up to 5 days.

pile o' waffles

MAKES 4 or 5 waffles
(recipe easily doubled)
PREP TIME 25 minutes, plus
chilling coconut milk overnight
COOK TIME 25 minutes

waffles

2 tablespoons ground flax

6 tablespoons water

2 cups whole wheat flour

2 tablespoons granulated sugar

1 teaspoon baking powder

½ teaspoon ground cinnamon

½ teaspoon sea salt

1 ½ cups nondairy milk

berry syrup

2 cups fresh or frozen mixed
berries

¼ cup maple syrup

whipped cream

2 (13.5 oz/400 ml) cans full-fat
coconut milk, refrigerated
overnight

2 tablespoons maple syrup

½ teaspoon ground cinnamon

A waffle iron is truly a brunch game changer, and it doesn't have to be an expensive investment. If you want to indulge in these whole wheat waffles or perhaps a potato waffle of some kind, any bargain you come across will get the job done. If you're looking to be efficient, you can pile up these bad boys, freeze 'em, and then pop 'em in a toaster or back in the waffle iron for reheating. You can also incorporate additions into the batter, like berries, bananas, vegan chocolate chips, or toasted nuts. For the whipped cream, I recommend using a chilled glass bowl and hand mixer.

To make the waffles, combine the flax and water together in a large bowl and set aside to thicken for 10 minutes while you preheat the waffle iron. Place a baking sheet in the oven and preheat to 200°F to keep the waffles warm.

Once the flax mixture has thickened, add the flour, sugar, baking powder, cinnamon, salt, and nondairy milk and fold until just combined. Be careful not to overmix the batter.

Lightly oil the waffle iron and add approximately ½ cup batter per waffle. Cook for 7 to 8 minutes. The time may vary depending on the make of your waffle iron. Transfer the finished waffles to the baking sheet in the oven.

Meanwhile, to make the berry syrup, heat up the berries and maple syrup in a saucepan over medium-low heat for 5 to 10 minutes until the berries are soft and warmed through.

Scoop the thick cream off the top of the cans of coconut milk and place in the bowl. Beat until smooth and fluffy. Fold in maple syrup and cinnamon.

Serve the waffles warm and top with the berry syrup and whipped cream.

If freezing the waffles, let cool completely. Layer them between parchment paper in a container or freezer bag, and consume within 1 month.

hot tip I have you using coconut cream a lot so if you can find cans that only contain the thick cream (a rare find) buy those, whereas if you use cans of full-fat coconut milk save the coconut water for sauces and smoothies. You can even freeze it for later use!

french toast coffee cake

MAKES 8 to 10 servings
PREP TIME 35 minutes, plus chilling coconut milk overnight
COOK TIME 35 minutes

french toast

- 1 cup nondairy milk
- ⅓ cup packed brown sugar
- ¼ cup chickpea flour
- 2 tablespoons nutritional yeast
- 2 tablespoons vegan butter, melted
- 1 teaspoon ground cinnamon
- ¼ teaspoon sea salt
- 7 cups cubed bread

cake batter

- 1 tablespoon ground flax
- 3 tablespoons water
- ⅓ cup nondairy milk
- ¼ cup packed brown sugar
- ¼ cup chickpea flour
- 2 tablespoons vegan butter, melted
- 1 tablespoon whole wheat or all-purpose flour

topping

- ¼ cup packed brown sugar
- ¼ cup whole wheat or all-purpose flour
- ¼ cup pecans, finely chopped
- ½ teaspoon ground cinnamon
- 2 tablespoons cold vegan butter, cubed

coffee-infused cream

- 2 (13.5 oz/400 ml) cans full-fat coconut milk, refrigerated overnight
- 2 tablespoons maple syrup
- ½ teaspoon instant coffee granules

Cake for breakfast . . . #goals! So have your cake and French toast all rolled into a breakfasty slice and devour it in the morning with a cup of coffee. Just pinch yourself to know you're not dreaming! I use a 9-inch springform pan so the cake can be removed easily, but if you don't have one, use a regular cake pan.

Preheat the oven to 350°F.

To make the French toast, combine the milk, sugar, flour, nutritional yeast, butter, cinnamon, and salt together in a large bowl. Add the cubed bread and allow it to soak.

Meanwhile, to make the cake batter, combine all the ingredients together in another bowl.

To make the topping, combine the sugar, flour, pecans, and cinnamon together in another bowl. Add the butter and pinch the ingredients together until you have a crumblike texture.

Lightly grease a 9-inch springform pan or cake pan. Press the soaked bread into the pan so it fills the pan to the edges and is well pressed together. Pour the cake batter evenly over the top, filling in the gaps between the bread. Spread the topping evenly on top.

Bake for 35 minutes or until a toothpick inserted in the center comes out clean. Let the cake cool for 15 to 20 minutes before removing the sides of the pan and lifting the cake off the bottom. If you've used a regular cake pan, your cake may come out clean and easily, or you can slice and serve the cake from the pan.

While the cake is cooling, make the coffee-infused cream. Scoop the thick cream off the top of the cans of coconut milk and place in a large chilled glass bowl. Beat with a mixer until fluffy and smooth. Fold in the maple syrup and instant coffee until combined.

Serve the cake slightly warm. Slice the cake and top each serving with the cream.

pumpkin spice pancakes

MAKES 10 pancakes
PREP TIME 20 minutes
COOK TIME 15-20 minutes

ingredients

1 cup all-purpose flour

½ cup whole wheat flour

½ teaspoon baking powder

½ teaspoon sea salt

½ teaspoon ground cinnamon

¼ teaspoon ground nutmeg

¼ teaspoon ground allspice

¼ teaspoon ground ginger

½ cup pure pumpkin puree

2 tablespoons maple syrup, plus more for serving

1½ to 2 cups nondairy milk

2 to 3 tablespoons vegan butter, for frying

Despite what the Internet tells me, my tastes aren't basic. I just love pumpkin spice, and I'm not ashamed. What I am is sick of all those memes giving it a bad reputation. Pumpkin spice combines all the best flavors, it works with just about anything sweet or savory, and if you make your own, you don't have to wait until fall to have your fix. This simple pancake batter marries real pumpkin puree with all its spicy sister wives—cinnamon, nutmeg, allspice, and ginger. I'd totally name my cats after those spices.

Heat a nonstick pan or griddle over medium-low heat and preheat the oven to 200°F. You'll place the pancakes on a baking sheet or plate in the oven to keep them warm while you cook.

In a bowl, combine the flours, baking powder, salt, and spices together with a whisk or fork. Add the pumpkin puree and maple syrup. Start by adding 1½ cups of the nondairy milk and stir together until the batter is well combined. It should be the consistency of a smoothie. You can thin it out a little more with milk if you prefer thinner pancakes.

Lightly butter the pan or griddle with vegan butter. Scoop out approximately ¼ cup batter for each pancake. Once the batter starts to bubble all around the pancake and the edges are slightly cooked through, then flip. Cook for approximately 2 to 3 minutes on each side. Be sure to adjust the heat as you go, as the pan will get really hot halfway through. Keep the cooked pancakes warm in the oven until all are ready.

Serve with more vegan butter and maple syrup!

finger foods

These finger lickin' good recipes keep it dirty and are meant to be devoured one bite at a time, no plates or forks necessary. If you're looking for appies to kick off a party or satisfy halftime grumbles, start here. You could also sit down on the couch and demolish one of these dishes all to yourself too—I ain't judging! And enough of these together makes a great grazing meal for a crowd.

hot buffalo chicken dip

MAKES 6 to 8 servings
PREP TIME 30 minutes
COOK TIME 35 minutes

ingredients

4 cups TVP or soy curl pieces

1 (16 oz/450 g) brick medium-firm tofu

2 cups finely diced onions (about 2 onions)

3 garlic cloves, minced

2 tablespoons vegetable oil

1½ cups vegan cream cheese

2 tablespoons nutritional yeast

2 tablespoons finely chopped chives

1 teaspoon chopped fresh dill

1 teaspoon apple cider vinegar

¾ teaspoon sea salt

½ teaspoon ground pepper

1 teaspoon chipotle chile powder

¾ cup buffalo-style hot sauce

1 cup vegan mozzarella or cheddar shreds

Vegetables, corn chips, crackers, or toasted bread of your choice, for serving

This is American comfort food at its best, and it's a dip that y'all have requested over and over again. I wasn't ignoring you, just saving it. It's creamy, hot, cheesy, and buffalo-y (I promise that's a real word . . . but don't look it up). It's also the perfect dip for any rager you're throwing or an excuse to pretend you care about the Superbowl! I wanted to offer up textured vegetable protein (TVP or soy curls) as a different option for vegan chicken that works well in this dip. If you're wondering, it is a soy flour product that has more protein than meat, so don't worry about where vegans get their protein, bro. But feel free to use your favorite meatless chicken product in place of this.

Preheat the oven to 350°F.

Soak the TVP in a bowl of tepid water for 10 minutes until spongy and doubled in size. Drain and squeeze out the excess water thoroughly through a strainer or sieve.

Meanwhile, drain the excess water from the tofu and pat dry with a tea towel or paper towel. Crumble the tofu. You will need 1¼ cups. The tofu doesn't need to be completely pressed or dry.

In a cast-iron skillet or oven-safe pan, sauté the onions and garlic over medium heat in 1 tablespoon of the vegetable oil for approximately 6 minutes until soft, translucent, and slightly golden. Lower the heat if necessary to prevent the garlic from burning.

Add the sautéed onions and garlic to a food processor along with the crumbled tofu, cream cheese, nutritional yeast, chives, dill, and vinegar. Season with ½ teaspoon of the salt and ¼ teaspoon of the pepper. Process until smooth.

In the same pan you used for the onions and garlic, brown the TVP pieces in the remaining 1 tablespoon of vegetable oil over medium heat for 3 minutes. Add ½ teaspoon of the chipotle chile powder and the remaining ¼ teaspoon each salt and pepper. Sauté for another 1 to 2 minutes until golden brown. Stir in the hot sauce and cook for another 4 to 5 minutes to make sure all the pieces are well coated in sauce. Turn off the heat.

CONTINUED

Fold the mixture from the food processor into the saucy TVP pieces in the pan. If the pan is oven-safe, you can bake and serve the dip in this, or transfer the mixture to a baking dish. Top with the cheese and sprinkle the remaining ½ teaspoon chipotle chile powder on top.

Bake for approximately 15 minutes. If the top is not browned to your liking, you can place the pan under the broiler for a couple of minutes. Watch it closely so the dip doesn't burn. Serve the dip warm from the oven with veggies, corn chips, crackers, or toasted bread of your choice. Refrigerate leftovers for up to 4 days. Reheat in the oven or microwave before serving.

herb-loaded sausage rolls

MAKES 40 pieces
PREP TIME 50 minutes
COOK TIME 25 minutes

prep ahead

The Maple-Mustard Dip
(page 210)

ingredients

1 cup sliced onion (about
1 onion)

2 cups sliced cremini
mushrooms (about 5 oz)

2 garlic cloves,
coarsely chopped

2 tablespoons olive oil

1 teaspoon fennel seeds

1 teaspoon dried or fresh
thyme leaves

½ teaspoon dried oregano

½ teaspoon dried sage

2 cups stemmed and coarsely
chopped kale

¾ cup cooked or canned navy
beans or white kidney beans,
rinsed and drained

2 teaspoons sea salt

1 teaspoon ground pepper

2 tablespoons nutritional yeast

½ cup vital wheat gluten

⅓ cup low-sodium vegetable
stock

½ cup packed fresh flat-leaf
parsley

1 package (1 lb/500 g) frozen
vegan puff pastry, thawed in
the fridge

¼ cup all-purpose flour, for
rolling out pastry

2 tablespoons vegan butter,
melted

The Maple-Mustard Dip,
for serving

WARNING: This recipe is pure gluten. There's gluten in the filling and gluten in the pastry. These might as well be called gluten rolls. Sorry, not sorry! They're freakin' tasty and were inspired by those little party appies you buy in a box. I can easily throw back twenty of these, no sweat, and I don't feel bad about it either 'cause there's also kale in them rolls.

In a large skillet, sauté the onion, mushrooms, and garlic in the olive oil over medium heat for 4 to 5 minutes until the mushrooms are soft and lightly browned. Add the fennel seeds, thyme, oregano, and sage and stir occasionally for another 3 to 4 minutes until the mixture is browned and cooked through. Toss in the kale during the last couple of minutes of cooking so the kale wilts but does not overcook. It should still appear bright green.

Add this mixture to a food processor with the beans, salt, pepper, nutritional yeast, vital wheat gluten, stock, and parsley. Process until the mixture comes together to form a ball of dough. It should be sticky and elastic to the touch. That indicates the gluten has activated and your mixture will be chewy in texture, sort of like sausage, when it's cooked in the puff pastry.

Some premade puff pastry is already rolled out thin and ready to use; others may need to be rolled out. Either way, place the pastry on a lightly floured surface. Roll as much as necessary with a floured rolling pin. Stop to check under the pastry and lightly flour again so it doesn't stick. You need a rectangle approximately 25 inches by 8 inches and ⅛ inch thick.

Cut the pastry across the 8-inch side into 5 strips approximately 4½ to 5 inches wide and 8 inches long. Form the filling in a log shape lengthwise on each strip of puff pastry. Fold the pastry over the mixture to form a roll 1 to 1¼ inches in diameter, using the overlap to seal the edge. Place the roll seam side down and slice crosswise into eight 1-inch pieces.

Line a baking sheet with parchment paper and arrange the rolls on the sheet spaced 1 inch apart. Chill in the fridge or freezer for 15 minutes before baking. At this point, you could also lightly flour the rolls, place

CONTINUED

between layers of parchment paper in a container or freezer bag, and freeze for later use.

Preheat the oven to 425°F.

Just before baking the rolls, brush the tops with the melted vegan butter. Bake for 14 to 16 minutes or until puffed, flaky, and golden in color. If baking frozen rolls, brush the tops with butter and bake for about 20 minutes. Serve warm with the dip.

cheesy pesto bread twists

MAKES 12 large or 24 small pieces
PREP TIME 40 minutes, plus up to
1 hour for proofing
COOK TIME 20 minutes

prep ahead

That Dough (page 168)
The Parm (page 207)

pesto

½ cup The Parm
3 cups packed fresh basil leaves
2 tablespoons freshly squeezed lemon juice
2 garlic cloves
¼ teaspoon ground pepper
¼ cup olive oil

bread twists

That Dough
¼ cup The Parm
2 teaspoons olive oil

I'm a junkie for pesto and obviously dough as well, so this is the best arrangement ever! I've twisted a simple pesto into That Dough, which you can learn all about on page 168. Ya that dough! You'll be a master baker in no time. I believe in you. But I'm warning you: these are extremely addictive and the kind of thing that will certainly ruin your dinner. I'm sure you're okay with that since you're an adult after all!

To make the pesto, combine The Parm, basil, lemon juice, garlic, and pepper in a food processor. Once it's running, drizzle in the olive oil and continue processing until smooth.

To make the bread twists, lightly flour a work surface and a rolling pin. Roll out the dough to a rectangle approximately 17 by 12 inches.

Spread the pesto on the dough out to the edges and sprinkle with The Parm.

Line 2 baking sheets with parchment paper.

Fold the dough in half lengthwise. If you want shorter twists, cut the folded rectangle in half lengthwise. Cut the dough crosswise into strips approximately 1½ inches wide. You should have 12 long strips or 24 short strips.

Hold each strip at either end and twist the ends in opposite directions a few times, revealing the layers of dough and pesto. Place the twists on the baking sheets spaced 1½ inches apart.

Brush the twists with the olive oil.

Cover the baking sheets with plastic wrap and a damp tea towel and allow the twists to rise in a warm, dark place until double in size. This could take 20 minutes to 1 hour depending on your environment.

When ready to bake, preheat the oven to 375°F.

Bake the twists for 20 minutes until golden brown.

The twists are best served immediately, while warm. You can freeze baked leftovers, once they are completely cooled, between layers of parchment paper. Use within 1 month. Warm the frozen twists in a 350°F oven for approximately 10 minutes.

zucchini-onion bhaji

MAKES 12 pieces
PREP TIME 45 minutes
COOK TIME 10 minutes

prep ahead

The Sour Cream (page 210)

ingredients

2 cups spiraled or grated
zucchini (about 1 large zucchini)

2¼ teaspoons sea salt

4 to 6 cups vegetable oil,
for frying

2 cups halved and thinly sliced
onions (about 2 onions)

½ teaspoon ground cumin

½ teaspoon paprika

½ teaspoon garam masala

¼ teaspoon chili powder

¼ teaspoon ground pepper

1¼ cups chickpea flour

1 teaspoon baking powder

¼ cup unsweetened nondairy
milk

1 tablespoon freshly squeezed
lemon juice

Cilantro leaves (optional),
for garnish

The Sour Cream

I have very fond memories of eating *bhajis*, which are delightful Indian snacks. I can get them at some of my favorite restaurants in Toronto—some Indian, some Thai, and at one time even a vegan British pub that has since closed. RIP Porter House. Essentially a *bhaji* is a fritter or sometimes is also called *pakora*, but I gotta stick to *bhaji* for nostalgia's sake! The ones I've had all have a base of onion and mixed in are different veggies from squash to eggplant, but the common denominator was that they were all magically delicious! I love them dipped into The Sour Cream (page 210), and I hope you enjoy sinking your teeth into these savory little guys as much as I do.

Place the zucchini in a bowl with 2 teaspoons of the salt and toss with your hands to coat well. Let sit for 30 minutes. Rinse the zucchini and squeeze out excess water through a sieve. Pat dry with a paper towel.

Heat vegetable oil in a large heavy-bottomed pot or fryer to a temperature of 350°F to 360°F on a deep-frying thermometer. The amount of oil may vary depending on the size of your vessel.

Add the zucchini to a large bowl with the sliced onions, remaining ¼ teaspoon salt, spices, chickpea flour, baking powder, nondairy milk, and lemon juice. Toss by hand, making sure the zucchini and onion are well coated.

Grab a small handful of the mixture (approximately ¼ cup) and gently place in the hot oil. Cook in small batches for 2 to 2½ minutes until deep golden brown. Remove with a slotted frying spoon onto paper towels to absorb excess oil. Garnish with the cilantro and serve immediately with sour cream for dipping.

baked jalapeño poppers

MAKES 4 to 6 servings
PREP TIME 40 minutes
COOK TIME 20 minutes

prep ahead

Tofu Bacon Crumbles (page 10)

The Sundried Tomato Aioli
(page 226)

ingredients

1 cup vegan cream cheese,
preferably flavored with herbs,
chives, or garlic

3 tablespoons finely chopped
chives

2 tablespoons cilantro, finely
chopped (optional)

1 garlic clove, minced

½ cup Tofu Bacon

7 to 10 jalapeño chile peppers
(depending on size)

½ cup bread crumbs

½ teaspoon smoked paprika
or chili powder

½ teaspoon garlic powder

½ teaspoon sea salt

Vegetable oil spray, for coating

The Sundried Tomato Aioli

A classic appie shouldn't be messed with too much so I kept these poppers pretty true to what you're used to, stuffing them with an herby cream cheese filling and bacon bits. They're just the right size to eat in one or two bites with your hands. If you're afraid of being eaten alive by the heat of a jalapeño, the key is cleaning out the middle seeds entirely, but as someone who walks on the mild side I find the cream cheese and The Sundried Tomato Aioli also helps soothe the heat while you eat!

Preheat the oven to 375°F.

Mix the cream cheese together with the chives, cilantro, garlic, and bacon crumbles in a bowl. Refrigerate while you prepare the jalapeños.

Cut the jalapeños in half lengthwise and gently scoop out the flesh and seeds with a small spoon or pairing knife, being sure not to break the peppers.

Combine the bread crumbs with the paprika, garlic powder, and salt in a shallow dish.

Line a baking sheet with parchment paper.

Stuff the jalapeño halves with the cream cheese mixture. Have some of the mixture slightly piling out of the halves but not overflowing. Sprinkle the tops with the bread crumb mixture, coating them well. Place on the baking sheet.

To help brown the tops, spray with a light coating of oil. Bake for 18 to 20 minutes until golden brown.

Serve immediately with a drizzle of the aioli on each piece or serve the aioli on the side as a dip.

southern fried cauliflower

SERVES 4 to 6
PREP TIME 25 minutes
COOK TIME 75 minutes

prep ahead

The Spicy Sriracha Aioli
(page 227)

cauliflower

8 to 9 cups cauliflower florets
(two-bite size)

2 tablespoons vegetable oil,
plus 4 to 6 cups for deep-frying

1 teaspoon sea salt

½ teaspoon ground pepper

The Spicy Sriracha Aioli, or the
dip of your choice

batter

1 cup unsweetened
nondairy milk

1 tablespoon apple cider vinegar

¼ cup buffalo-style hot sauce

2 teaspoons cornstarch

2 cups all-purpose flour

1 tablespoon sea salt

1 tablespoon chili powder

2 teaspoons garlic powder

2 teaspoons onion powder

1 teaspoon ground pepper

1 teaspoon ground sage

1 teaspoon ground coriander

1 teaspoon smoked paprika

1 teaspoon celery salt

½ teaspoon ground nutmeg

½ teaspoon ground cinnamon

½ teaspoon ground cumin

½ teaspoon ground allspice

Our extremely popular buffalo cauliflower inspired this jacked-up version that's going to bring back all your regretful carnivorous memories of fried chicken! It doesn't get more comforting than this. (Well it does, 'cause you're only two chapters into the book.) I really like this as meaty two-bite pieces, but you could also go for popcorn style or try chicken fried steak style by slicing your cauliflower the way we do with the Buffalo Cauliflower Sandwich (page 103). Serve it up with peas, mashed potatoes, and The Gravy (page 220), and you've got yourself one helluva Southern classic!

Preheat the oven to 425°F.

To prepare the cauliflower, toss the cauliflower on a baking sheet with the 2 tablespoons vegetable oil, salt, and ground pepper. Bake for 30 to 35 minutes until tender. Let cool if necessary before handling the florets for battering.

Heat the oil for deep-frying in a large heavy-bottomed pot or deep fryer to a temperature of 325°F to 350°F on a deep-frying thermometer. The amount of oil may vary depending on the size of your frying vessel.

To make the batter, combine the nondairy milk with the apple cider vinegar and hot sauce in a large bowl. Mix the cornstarch with a small amount of the milk mixture to make a slurry and add to the bowl. This helps avoid lumps.

In another large bowl, combine the flour with the salt and all the spices.

Do not batter the cauliflower and let it sit before it goes in the oil. Only coat the pieces once the oil has reached 325°F. Batter a floret, then coat in the flour mixture, then submerge in the batter again and coat in the flour mixture once again. Fry a few pieces at a time for 4 to 5 minutes until golden brown and crispy.

Remove with a slotted frying spoon onto a baking sheet or large plate covered with paper towels to absorb excess oil.

Serve with the aioli or a dip of your choice.

To reheat leftover fried cauliflower, place the pieces on a baking sheet and bake in a 425°F oven for 10 to 12 minutes.

hot tip I prefer these rings deep-fried, but you can bake them if you make the filling from scratch. If you're using leftover Bacon Mac & Cheese Skillet (page 131), you'll definitely need to deep-fry the rings or the filling will get overcooked. If baking the rings, arrange on parchment-lined baking sheets. I recommend spraying the breaded rings with a light coating of oil. Bake in a preheated 400°F oven for 30 minutes, flipping the rings halfway through the bake time.

mac & cheese onion rings

MAKES 6 to 8 servings
PREP TIME 20 minutes, plus 1 to 2 hours for freezing rings
COOK TIME 50 minutes

prep ahead

Mac & Cheese Sauce (page 131)

ingredients

2½ cups elbow macaroni

Mac & Cheese Sauce

5 or 6 (2¼-inch) onions

4 to 6 cups vegetable oil, for deep-frying

4 cups panko-style bread crumbs

2 teaspoons dried oregano

2 teaspoons dried basil

2 teaspoons sea salt

1 teaspoon chili powder

1½ cups all-purpose flour

1¾ cups unsweetened nondairy milk

2 teaspoons egg replacer powder or cornstarch

Hot sauce or ketchup, for dipping

You're not dreaming—what you're looking at is for real! I've managed to merge two of my favorite things into one drool-worthy morsel. It's creamy mac and cheese stuffed into onion rings, then deep-fried with a crispy seasoned bread crumb coating.

In a large pot of salted boiling water, cook the macaroni until al dente. Drain but do not rinse. Combine the cooked macaroni with the sauce in a large bowl just before assembling the onion rings. You can also cook the noodles and make the sauce ahead of time but don't combine them until you're ready to assemble the onion rings.

Line 2 baking sheets with parchment paper. Trim the ends of each whole onion so they're flat end to end. Then cut the onions into slices approximately ¾ inch thick. Separate the slices into rings and lay them out on the baking sheets.

Fill each ring generously with the sauced macaroni, leaving no gaps and leveling it out on top. The filling shouldn't be mounding beyond the onion ring. Freeze for 1 to 2 hours or until the sauce has solidified. It doesn't need to be rock-solid frozen, but solid enough that nothing falls out when you lift a ring.

When ready to fry, heat the oil in a large heavy-bottomed pot or deep fryer to a temperature of 350°F to 360°F on a deep-frying thermometer.

In a bowl, combine the bread crumbs with the oregano, basil, 1½ teaspoon of the salt, and the chili powder. In another bowl, stir together the flour, nondairy milk, egg replacer, and remaining ½ teaspoon salt to make a smooth batter.

Coat a frozen ring in the batter, allowing the excess to drip off, then right away coat evenly with the bread crumb mixture.

Work with a few batches at a time and fry immediately for 3 to 4 minutes for large rings and 2½ to 3 minutes for smaller rings. Flip the pieces halfway through frying. Remove them with a slotted frying spoon onto baking sheets lined with paper towels.

The rings are best served immediately with hot sauce or ketchup for dipping. They're also great left over and cold, or you can reheat them in an oven or microwave until warmed through.

spicy black bean taquitos

SERVES 4 to 6
PREP TIME 45 minutes
COOK TIME 15-20 minutes

prep ahead

The Nacho Cheese (page 205)

The Guac Sauce (page 209)

The Sour Cream (page 210)

ingredients

1 small onion, halved

6 green onions, white and green parts, coarsely chopped

4 garlic cloves

½ teaspoon ground cumin

1 teaspoon chili powder

2 cups cooked black beans, or 1 can (19 oz/539 g) black beans, rinsed and drained

1 jalapeño chile pepper, seeded and diced (use half a jalapeño for mild)

1 cup thawed frozen corn

½ cup diced red bell pepper (about ½ pepper)

3 teaspoons vegetable oil, plus ½ cup for frying

1½ cups The Nacho Cheese

20 (6-inch) corn tortillas

The Guac Sauce, for serving

The Sour Cream, for serving

These black bean taquitos are a fun and easy party dish or can even make a great main event if you serve them with toppings like shredded lettuce, chopped tomato or salsa, and a chunkier guacamole. Yes, I'm suggesting you make a taquito salad. You can thank me later!

Process the onion halves, green onions, garlic, cumin, and chili powder in a food processor until very finely minced. Add the beans, jalapeño, corn, and bell pepper, and run the food processor a few times just to get everything very finely chopped, but don't process so much that the mixture becomes a smooth mash.

Heat a large cast-iron skillet or heavy-bottomed pan over medium heat with 1 teaspoon of the vegetable oil. Add the mixture from the food processor and cook for 3 to 4 minutes, stirring occasionally, until soft and fragrant.

Pour the mixture into a large bowl. Add the cheese and stir to combine well.

Wipe out the skillet and coat it with 1 teaspoon of the vegetable oil heated over medium-low heat. Place 2 to 3 tortillas in the pan to warm up, flipping once or twice. This step may be unnecessary if you're using flour tortillas or have very fresh corn tortillas. I always find they're a little dry, and this will help with rolling the taquitos. Add the remaining 1 teaspoon vegetable oil to the pan after warming a few tortillas, if necessary. As you remove the warmed tortillas from the pan, start rolling them up. Place about 2 tablespoons of filling on one-third of a tortilla and shape into a log, rolling tightly and tucking one end under. Place the filled tortillas seam side down on baking sheets.

Once all the tortillas are warmed, leave the pan over the heat and add the ½ cup vegetable oil for frying.

Place the taquitos seam side down in the hot frying oil. They should sizzle immediately or else the oil isn't hot enough. Fry in batches for 3 to 4 minutes, flipping the taquitos halfway through. Lower the heat if necessary. Remove the fried taquitos to paper towels to absorb excess oil.

Serve immediately with The Guac Sauce and sour cream.

hot tip I very much prefer deep-fried taquitos, but if you must bake them, preheat the oven to 400°F. There is no need to cook the filling before baking. Place the rolled taquitos seam side down on parchment-lined baking sheets. Spray with a light coating of oil and bake for 15 minutes, flipping the taquitos halfway through the bake time, until golden and slightly crisp. They will not get as crispy as the deep-fried version!

crispy crabless cakes

MAKES 10 cakes
PREP TIME 30 minutes
COOK TIME 15 minutes

prep ahead

The Horseradish-Dill Aioli
(page 226)

crabless cakes

2 cups drained marinated
artichoke hearts, finely chopped,
plus 2 tablespoons liquid

¼ cup finely chopped shallot
(about 1 small shallot)

½ cup finely chopped celery
(about 1 stalk)

1 teaspoon freshly squeezed
lemon juice

½ cup chickpea flour

2 teaspoons coconut sugar
or brown sugar

1 teaspoon Old Bay seasoning

¼ teaspoon sea salt

¼ teaspoon ground pepper

1 to 2 cups vegetable oil,
for frying

The Horseradish-Dill Aioli

breading

¼ cup chickpea flour

1¼ cups multigrain bread
crumbs

½ cup unsweetened
nondairy milk

The first time I had a vegan crab cake I was shook! John and I were eating at Lakeside (Wynn Hotel) in Las Vegas and devoured chef Tal Ronnen's crab cakes in seconds. There was no way I could get access to his secret recipe, but I carefully examined every bite so I could figure it out at home. There are a lot of vegan crab cake recipes made from artichokes or hearts of palm floating around the Internet, and while they're all pretty delicious, ours has been tried and tested by many former seafood addicts who claim they'd rather eat this than the real thing any day!

To make the crabless cakes, place all the ingredients except the oil and aioli in a large bowl. Combine well with a fork. It's important that the artichokes, shallots, and celery are very small and uniformly chopped so that the cakes will stick together while frying.

You should have a ½ inch of vegetable oil in a large cast-iron skillet or other heavy-bottomed pan for frying. Heat it to a temperature of 350°F to 360°F on a deep-frying thermometer.

To make the breading, place the chickpea flour in a wide, shallow dish. Use another shallow dish for the bread crumbs and a bowl for the milk.

Take ¼ cup of the crabless cake mixture and press and form it into a thick patty with your hands. Gently place the cake in the chickpea flour and coat all sides evenly. Quickly submerge it in milk and make sure all the flour looks wet. Remove it from the milk and place in the bread crumbs. Using your hands, coat all sides of the cake well in the bread crumbs, then lightly shake off any excess. Set the coated cakes on a plate or baking sheet. Once they're all assembled, immediately deep-fry in batches.

Delicately place 2 or 3 cakes in the hot oil. Fry for about 4 minutes until golden brown, flipping halfway through. Gently remove the cakes with a slotted frying spoon and place on paper towels to absorb any excess oil.

Serve immediately with the aioli. Leftovers can be heated over medium heat in a pan lightly coated with vegetable oil.

veggie sides & big salads

Not including too many salads or raw vegetables in this cookbook was completely intentional. Comfort food really needs to be warm! But I do love transforming vegetables and elevating their flavor, so here are a few lighter ideas for when you need a break from all the robust recipes. Vegetables are always the stars in vegan cooking, but here they shine bright in all their colorful glory! And they still feel indulgent, not pious, I promise.

lemony parm green beans

SERVES 4 to 6
PREP TIME 15 minutes
COOK TIME 10 minutes

prep ahead

The Parm (page 207)

ingredients

2 pounds green beans

2 teaspoons olive oil

1 shallot, finely sliced

Juice of ½ lemon, plus grated zest from 1 lemon

Sea salt and ground pepper

¼ cup The Parm

This is how I grew up eating green beans. For all I know my mom got this recipe from a magazine in the late '80s, but it remains my favorite way to eat my veggies. The lemon brings a fresh brightness to this dish, and if it lights you up, give it a try on broccoli, cauliflower, snow peas, or kale too!

Wash the green beans and trim the stems.

Heat a large cast-iron skillet or heavy-bottomed pan over medium heat. When it's hot, add the olive oil and green beans. Sauté for 4 to 5 minutes, tossing occasionally.

Add the shallot and continue to cook for 3 to 4 minutes, again only tossing occasionally, allowing the shallots to caramelize.

Add the lemon juice and salt and pepper to taste and cook for another minute or so. The beans should be bright green and not overcooked or too wilted.

Turn off the heat and add the lemon zest and The Parm and toss to coat well.

Serve immediately in the pan or arrange on a serving platter.

mushroom & herb toast

MAKES 4 servings
PREP TIME 25 minutes
COOK TIME 10 minutes

prep ahead

The Parm (page 207)

ingredients

8 ounces chanterelle mushrooms

8 ounces shiitake mushrooms

4 tablespoons olive oil

½ teaspoon finely chopped fresh rosemary

½ teaspoon fresh thyme leaves

2 tablespoons finely chopped fresh flat-leaf parsley

¼ cup white wine

¼ teaspoon sea salt

¼ teaspoon ground pepper

1 tablespoon freshly squeezed lemon juice

4 slices sourdough bread

¼ cup The Parm

Mushrooms are truly a magical culinary gift. Their earthy flavor and hearty texture make them absolutely one of my favorite ingredients. Here I use shiitakes and chanterelles, and when you try this you'll understand why these fancy varieties attract all the attention like the fun guys they are! They get a quick sauté in fresh herbs and are served mounded on scrumptious sourdough.

Preheat the oven to 450°F if toasting the bread in the oven.

Do not wash the mushrooms under running water; rather, take a damp cloth or paper towel and brush off any visible dirt or debris. Trim the bottom ¼ inch of the chanterelle stems and trim the woody part of the shiitake stems if necessary. Slice the chanterelles and any large shiitakes. If the shiitakes are fairly small, I prefer leaving them whole.

Heat a cast-iron skillet or frying pan over medium heat with 2 tablespoons of the olive oil. Sauté the mushrooms with the rosemary, thyme, and parsley for about 4 minutes. Add the white wine, salt, and pepper and cook for another 2 to 3 minutes until most of the liquid is evaporated.

Add the lemon juice and cook for 1 minute.

Meanwhile, brush the sourdough slices with the remaining 2 tablespoons olive oil and either grill oil side down in a grill pan or toast oil side up on a baking sheet in the oven until golden brown.

Top each slice with a mound of mushrooms and garnish with about 1 tablespoon of The Parm. Serve immediately!

green curry cauliflower roast

MAKES 4 to 6 servings
PREP TIME 20 minutes
COOK TIME 55 minutes

ingredients

½ cup finely chopped onion (about ½ onion)

2 garlic cloves, minced

2 tablespoons vegetable oil

1 can (13.5 oz/400 ml) full-fat coconut milk

3 kaffir lime leaves

2 tablespoons coarsely chopped Thai basil

1 tablespoon maple syrup

2 tablespoons green curry paste

½ teaspoon sea salt

1 tablespoon freshly squeezed lime juice

1 large cauliflower

My love for the cauli will never die! It's the blandest-looking vegetable of the bunch and yet has so much flavor hidden away in its deepest corners. Of course, you could cut it up, baste it, and roast it in anything you want, but there's something about the way a whole cauliflower looks when roasted and caramelized. Honestly, it's just sexy! Plus now you don't have a bunch of cutting to do! This version is done green curry–style, and I like it on its own or served in slabs over brown rice.

Preheat the oven to 400°F.

In a cast-iron skillet or oven-safe pan over medium heat, sauté the onion and garlic in the vegetable oil for approximately 3 minutes until just softened, lowering the heat if necessary to prevent the garlic from burning. Stir in the coconut milk, lime leaves, basil, maple syrup, curry paste, salt, and lime juice. Bring to a simmer and cook for 4 to 5 minutes until the curry mixture thickens slightly.

Meanwhile, trim all the leaves from the base of the cauliflower. Trim the thick part of the stalk as much as necessary so the cauliflower can sit flat in the skillet.

Place the cauliflower bottom side up in the skillet and pour half of the curry mixture onto the bottom, allowing it to seep into the cauliflower florets for a minute. Then flip it right side up and pour the remaining curry mixture over top. The excess will pool around the cauliflower. Use a brush to coat all parts of the cauliflower.

Roast for 45 minutes, basting once or twice during the bake time, until tender and a golden caramelized color forms on the outside of the cauliflower.

Carve into thick slices and serve immediately.

brussels sprouts caesar salad

MAKES 2 entrée or
4 appetizer servings
PREP TIME 30 minutes
COOK TIME 45 minutes

prep ahead

Almond Bacon (page 10)

The Parm (page 207)

caesar dressing

1 garlic bulb

3 teaspoons olive oil

2 pinches plus 1 teaspoon sea salt

¾ cup raw cashews, soaked in hot water for 20 minutes

¾ cup water

1 pitted medjool date

3½ tablespoons nutritional yeast

1 teaspoon grated lemon zest

3 tablespoons freshly squeezed lemon juice

1 tablespoon apple cider vinegar

1 teaspoon ground pepper

½ teaspoon Dijon mustard

brussels sprouts

2 tablespoons olive oil

2½ pounds brussels sprouts, halved (about 10 cups)

1 teaspoon sea salt

½ teaspoon ground pepper

2 tablespoons capers

1 cup Almond Bacon

¼ cup The Parm

Lemon wedges, for serving

Team warm salads unite! Roasted veggies make salads feel cozier and make me feel satisfied no matter what the season. In the summer you can grill the vegetables on the barbecue. Here I've modified our original kale Caesar salad recipe into a hearty filling Caesar salad with roasted brussels sprouts as the base.

Preheat the oven to 400°F.

To prepare the dressing, peel any excess layers of skin from the garlic bulb, leaving some skin intact. Cut the bulb in half crosswise to expose the cloves. Coat each half with 1½ teaspoons of the olive oil and sprinkle with a pinch of salt. Place in a small baking pan and bake for 35 minutes until the cloves are browned and very soft to touch.

Remove the roasted cloves from the bulb and place in a high-powered blender.

Drain and rinse the cashews. Add the cashews and the remaining ingredients to the blender and process on high until very smooth.

You can make the dressing ahead and refrigerate it. But since this salad is meant to be served warm, allow the dressing to sit at room temperature before serving to take the chill off. If you make it fresh with the roasted garlic, the dressing will be slightly warm already and can be served on the salad immediately.

To prepare the brussels sprouts, heat a large cast-iron skillet or frying pan over medium-high heat. Once the pan is hot, add the olive oil, brussels sprouts, salt, and ground pepper. Cook for 10 to 12 minutes, stirring occasionally, to develop some golden brown color.

In a bowl, toss the warm brussels sprouts with the capers and ½ cup of the dressing until well combined. Top with the bacon and The Parm and serve with extra dressing and lemon wedges. This salad is nice served with toasted or grilled sourdough topped with vegan butter as well.

banh mi bowl

MAKES 4 servings
PREP TIME 30 minutes
COOK TIME 50 minutes

prep ahead

The Jalapeño-Lime Aioli
(page 227)

The BBQ Sauce (page 209)

ingredients

1 (16 oz/450 g) brick medium-firm or firm tofu

2 tablespoons cornstarch

½ cup The BBQ Sauce or store-bought sauce

4 cups stemmed and shredded or finely chopped kale

4 cups shredded or finely chopped napa cabbage

¼ cup The Jalapeño-Lime Aioli, plus more for drizzling

3 green onions, white and green parts, coarsely chopped (½ cup)

2 cups shredded or ribboned carrot (about 1 large carrot)

2 cups shredded or ribboned English cucumber (about 1 cucumber)

1 cup packed coarsely chopped cilantro

½ cup sliced pickled or fresh jalapeño chile peppers

Here you have a deconstructed Vietnamese sandwich known as a *banh mi*. That doesn't mean that this bowl couldn't very well get dressed up with a baguette to become a sandwich once again. Just slice the tofu instead of cubing it. That's how many of the recipes in this book work once you're familiar with them; you can use them interchangeably and tweak them to your taste. When you get to the Stacked Sandwiches chapter (page 90), you'll see how even many of those components can transition back to salads. The only limit is your imagination.

Preheat the oven to 425°F.

Drain the excess water from the tofu and pat dry with a tea towel or paper towels. Cut into small cubes. Toss the cubes in the cornstarch and lay out on a baking sheet, spacing the cubes ¼ inch apart. Bake for 30 to 40 minutes until golden and crispy. There isn't really a need to flip the pieces while baking unless you find your oven bakes unevenly.

Toss the crispy tofu in the BBQ sauce in a bowl. Lay out the cubes on the baking sheet, spacing them ¼ inch apart once again. Reserve any excess sauce to toss with the tofu just before assembling the bowls. Bake for 10 minutes.

To assemble the bowls, toss the kale and cabbage together in a large bowl with the aioli and the chopped green onions. Toss to coat well.

Place the dressed greens in serving bowls. Top with the carrot, cucumber, cilantro, jalapeños, and tofu. Drizzle with more aioli, if desired.

hot tip If you want more pickle, top the bowls with Pickled Red Onions (page 107) and/or submerge the carrot and cucumber in equal parts rice vinegar and warm water, with 1 teaspoon each sugar and salt. Let sit for 20 minutes.

my big fat greek potato salad

MAKES 6 to 8 servings
PREP TIME 45 minutes, plus
marinating for 3 hours or overnight
COOK TIME 45 minutes

prep ahead

The Creamy Cucumber
(page 223)

tofu feta

1 (14 oz/390 g) brick firm
or extra-firm tofu

½ cup white wine vinegar

1 tablespoon freshly squeezed
lemon juice

½ cup unsweetened soy
or almond milk

1 teaspoon dried basil

2 garlic cloves, minced

2 teaspoons sea salt

salad

2 pounds small white or red
potatoes, halved

1 tablespoon olive oil

1 teaspoon dried oregano

½ teaspoon sea salt

½ teaspoon ground pepper

2 cups diced English cucumber
(about 1 cucumber)

2 cups diced green bell pepper
(about 2 peppers)

2 cups cherry tomatoes, halved

2 cups diced red onion (about
2 onions)

½ cup pitted kalamata olives

6 to 8 pepperoncini peppers

The Creamy Cucumber

Dried oregano, for serving

This is a potato salad with substance, and it'll get you stoked for a beach day or picnic with your pals. It's got chunks of all things Greek and is a welcome change from the typical variation. You could even swap rotini or macaroni for the potatoes for a big fat Greek pasta salad.

To prepare the tofu feta, drain the excess water from the tofu and pat and press it dry between paper towels or a tea towel. You don't need to get all the water out, just some of it. Cut the tofu into ½-inch cubes.

Whisk together the vinegar, lemon juice, nondairy milk, basil, garlic, and salt in a glass container with a fitted lid. Submerge the tofu cubes in the mixture, place the lid on the container, and refrigerate. Marinate the tofu overnight for a strong flavor, but you can marinate it for as little as 3 hours.

To prepare the salad, preheat the oven to 400°F.

Toss the potatoes in the olive oil, oregano, salt, and pepper in a baking dish. Bake for 45 minutes, tossing once halfway through the bake time, until roasted and golden brown.

Toss the warm potatoes with the cucumber, bell pepper, tomatoes, onion, olives, pepperoncini, and tofu feta. Drizzle with as much creamy cucumber dressing as you like and serve immediately. Add extra ground pepper and/or oregano to taste.

Be sure to dress only the amount you will consume. If you're not eating the salad right away, do not toss the potatoes with the veggies, as the cucumber and tomatoes will get soggy.

southwest chop salad

MAKES 4 servings
PREP TIME 25 minutes

prep ahead

The Classic Ranch (page 223)

Coconut Bacon (page 9)

ingredients

8 cups finely chopped romaine lettuce (1 large head)

1 cup finely chopped red onion (about 1 onion)

2 cups fresh or frozen and thawed corn kernels

2 cups cooked black beans, or 1 can (19 oz/539 g) black beans, rinsed and drained

2 cups cherry tomatoes, halved

1 large avocado, pitted, peeled, and diced

1 cup Coconut Bacon

The Classic Ranch

This is a fast and fresh salad that I rely on often. Usually I prep all the components ahead of time and store everything separately so I'm ready for quick assembly throughout the week. That's about as organized as I get when it comes to nourishing myself, so this is what I turn to when I need to reset. And if you didn't notice, this salad also gifts you with the makings of a pretty nice veggie taco too!

Assemble each salad with 2 cups of the chopped romaine, ¼ cup of the diced onion, and ½ cup each of the corn, beans, and tomatoes, plus one-fourth of the avocado.

Top with the bacon and ranch dressing. Feel free to go wild on those two things too!

hot tip Wanna make this salad warm? Sauté the black beans, corn, and red onion together with the spices of your choice, and leave the rest of the ingredients raw and fresh. Ummm, also taco worthy!

hearty soups

This chapter is like taking a leisurely stroll down the canned soup aisle at the grocery store and throwing everything into your cart. Maybe one day we'll live in a world where vegans could actually do that without worrying about the ingredient list, but even if we could, nothing compares to homemade. To make soups efficiently, chop and prep all your ingredients in advance so you're just throwing stuff into the pot at the right time and not overcooking or undercooking ingredients. These hearty soups are comforting, clean, and cozy so slurp 'em up with pride and use them as inspo to concoct your own from-scratch soups whenever the urge strikes!

hot tip This recipe will probably leave you with unused puff pastry. The benefit of not using real butter or animal lard is you can you can refreeze it! Roll it out to ⅛ inch thick and place between plastic wrap. Fold it over itself and place in the freezer for another use. Thaw before using once again.

chicken potpie soup

MAKES 6 servings
PREP TIME 1 hour
COOK TIME 35 minutes

ingredients

2 cups peeled and diced white or yellow potatoes (about 2 potatoes)

2 tablespoons arrowroot flour or all-purpose flour

2 cups unsweetened soy milk

2 tablespoons vegetable oil

2 cups finely chopped meatless chicken

1 cup finely chopped onion (about 1 onion)

1 cup finely chopped carrot (about 1 large carrot)

1 cup finely chopped celery (about 2 stalks)

3 garlic cloves, minced

1 teaspoon mustard powder

1 teaspoon fresh thyme

½ teaspoon ground basil

½ teaspoon ground sage

½ teaspoon sea salt

½ teaspoon ground pepper

1 vegan chicken-flavored bouillon cube dissolved in 2 cups water, or 2 cups low-sodium vegetable stock

1 cup fresh or frozen corn

1 cup fresh or frozen peas

¼ cup packed fresh flat-leaf parsley, finely chopped

1 (1 lb/500 g) package frozen vegan puff pastry, thawed in the fridge

¼ cup all-purpose flour, for rolling out pastry

I don't want to argue about whether this is a chicken potpie or a chicken potpie soup. It's both! But the chicken potpies I recall eating when the babysitter was over—which were from a box BTW—had the thickest, gooiest filling that I didn't find that appetizing. So I thinned it out to my liking and called it soup! It's my book, and I can do what I want. Regardless, it's spot-on and delish. You can ditch the puff pastry topping and pair the soup with Flaky Buttermilk Biscuits (page 15) or a crusty loaf of bread for dipping.

Bring a pot of cold water and the potatoes to a boil and cook for 8 to 10 minutes until tender. Drain and add 1 cup of the potatoes to a high-powered blender with the arrowroot flour and soy milk. Blend until smooth and set aside.

Preheat the oven to 425°F.

Heat a large stockpot over medium heat with the vegetable oil and sauté the meatless chicken for about 4 minutes until lightly browned. Add the onion, carrot, celery, garlic, mustard, thyme, basil, sage, salt, and pepper. Sauté for 5 minutes, stirring occasionally, until the veggies are softened and half cooked.

Add a bit of stock to lift the brown bits off the bottom of the pot. Slowly add the blended potato mixture, bring to a low simmer, and stir constantly while it thickens slightly. Add the remaining stock, remaining potatoes, corn, peas, and parsley. Bring to a simmer and cook for 5 minutes. Turn off the heat and cover the pot while you prepare the puff pastry.

Some premade puff pastry is already rolled out thin and ready to use; others may need to be rolled out. Either way, place the pastry on a lightly floured surface. Roll out with a floured rolling pin to ⅛ inch thick. Stop to check under the pastry and lightly flour again so it doesn't stick. Use oven-safe bowls or ramekins for the soup. Trace circles on the pastry ¼ inch larger than the bowls and cut out the circles.

Ladle the soup into the bowls and place the bowls on a baking sheet. Brush the edges of each bowl with a bit of soup and place a pastry round on top, gently pressing the edges to seal.

Bake for 10 to 12 minutes until the pastry is golden brown and puffed. Serve immediately!

real wonton soup

MAKES 4 servings;
35 to 40 wontons
PREP TIME 50 minutes
COOK TIME 10 minutes

wontons

4 ounces shiitake mushrooms, stemmed

½ large carrot, peeled

2 garlic cloves

1 green onion, white and green parts

¾ cup crumbled medium-firm tofu

1 teaspoon sea salt

¼ teaspoon smoked paprika

2 teaspoons toasted sesame oil

2 teaspoons seasoned rice vinegar

35 to 40 vegan wonton wrappers

broth

1 tablespoon toasted sesame oil, plus more if desired for serving

6 green onions, white and green parts, finely chopped and kept separate

1 tablespoon minced or grated ginger

2 garlic cloves, minced

4 cups shredded or finely chopped napa cabbage

1 tablespoon seasoned rice vinegar

1 tablespoon vegetarian oyster sauce or low-sodium tamari or soy sauce

4 cups low-sodium vegetable stock

2 cups water

1 teaspoon sea salt

This wonton soup is one of my favorite things in the book. It's highly satisfying and flavorful and tastes spot-on to restaurant-style wonton soup, with a simple gingery broth and dumplings filled with shiitake mushrooms and tofu. I have a special place for it in my comfort food memory bank because it essentially fueled me during the final months of the writing process! What's also magnificent is that the broth and wontons are easy to freeze so you can have this soup at the ready whenever you need to warm up your tummy.

To make the wontons, it's best to use a food processor for the filling, as the ingredients need to be finely minced. Mince the mushrooms, carrot, garlic, and green onion in the food processor. Add to a bowl.

Add the tofu, salt, paprika, sesame oil, and vinegar to the minced vegetables. Stir to combine well. The filling can be made in advance and left in the fridge overnight if you want to prep ahead.

Get a small bowl of water for sealing the wontons. Place about 2 scant teaspoons filling in the center of a wonton wrapper. Wet half of the edge of the wrapper and fold into a half-moon shape, pressing the wrapper and trying to remove any excess air around the edges and in the filling. If using square wrappers, fold into a triangle. Pinch the corners, lift the wonton slightly, and use an index finger to gently press into the bottom center as you slightly overlap and pinch together the two corners. Use an extra dab of water if needed to help the corners stick together. The final result will look like a tortellini. Lay each finished wonton on a lightly floured baking sheet and cover with a tea towel as you assemble them all. Leave covered while you make the broth.

Bring a pot of water to a rolling boil for cooking the wontons.

To make the broth, add the sesame oil to a stockpot over medium heat and sauté the white parts of the green onion, ginger, and garlic for 2 minutes until just softened and fragrant. Add the cabbage and continue to sauté for 2 minutes. Lower the heat if necessary to prevent the garlic from burning.

CONTINUED

Stir in the vinegar and oyster sauce and cook for 1 minute. Add the vegetable stock, water, and salt. Cover, bring to a simmer, and cook for 5 minutes.

Meanwhile, add the wontons to the pot of boiling water. They will take about 2 minutes to cook. Once they float to the surface, they're done. Remove them with a slotted spoon to serving bowls (9 or 10 wontons per serving).

Add the broth to each serving bowl. Top with the green parts of the green onions and extra sesame oil, if desired.

You can freeze the uncooked wontons between layers of parchment paper in a container or freezer bag for up to 2 months. Boil the frozen wontons, without thawing, per the instructions.

hot tip Medium-firm tofu is the best texture for the filling, but if you can't find it, you can use firm. If your crumbled tofu seems quite wet, drain it by squeezing out excess water through a fine-mesh nylon sieve, nut milk bag, or double layer of cheesecloth.

gooey french onion soup

MAKES 4 to 6 servings
PREP TIME 25 minutes
COOK TIME 75 minutes

prep ahead

The Mozza (page 208)

onion soup

6 cups thinly sliced onions
(about 6 onions)

¼ cup vegan butter

2 bay leaves

1 tablespoon fresh thyme leaves

1 to 2 teaspoons sea salt

½ teaspoon ground pepper

2 garlic cloves, minced

1 tablespoon all-purpose flour

2 tablespoons vegan
Worcestershire

¾ cup dry white wine or low-
sodium vegetable stock

2 vegan beef-flavored bouillon
cubes dissolved in 6 cups hot
water, or 6 cups low-sodium
vegetable stock

croutons

4 to 6 thick slices of baguette

The Mozza

Fresh thyme leaves, for garnish

This soup is such a classic comfort and one of the easiest to make. Getting the flavors balanced just right for a simple but rich onion broth is easy . . . it's cutting all the onions that'll have you in tears! But the water works are so worth it once you slurp up your first hot spoonful and bite into the sopped up crouton with gooey vegan mozza on top.

To make the soup, in a large stockpot over medium heat, sauté the onions with the butter for 3 to 4 minutes until soft and fragrant. Add the bay leaves, thyme, salt, and pepper and continue to cook for 12 to 15 minutes, stirring occasionally. If you're using vegan beef-flavored bouillon instead of vegetable stock, reduce the amount of salt you add here and, if necessary, adjust to taste afterward.

Once the onions are caramelized to a pale brown, reduce the heat to medium-low, add the garlic, and continue to cook, stirring occasionally, for 15 minutes.

Stir in the flour and Worcestershire, stir to coat the onions well, and cook for 2 minutes, stirring constantly.

Add the white wine, increase the heat to get it simmering, and cook for 2 minutes. You can use stock in place of the wine, but the wine makes the soup especially delicious!

Add the stock and bring to a boil, then lower the heat and simmer for 30 minutes.

While the soup is simmering, make the croutons.

Preheat the oven to 350°F.

The baguette slices should be a size that will fit submerged in your soup bowls. Place the slices on a baking sheet and toast in the oven for 15 to 18 minutes, flipping them halfway through the bake time. The toast should be quite hard and crusty. Set the croutons aside.

Set the oven to broil. Place oven-safe bowls on the baking sheet and ladle out the soup. Place a crouton on top slightly submerged in the soup but

CONTINUED

still floating and visible. Generously spoon some of The Mozza on top of the crouton. Some can go onto the soup out to the edges of each bowl. Set the baking sheet under the broiler and broil for 3 to 5 minutes until The Mozza is golden brown and slightly bubbling. Watch closely so it doesn't burn!

Garnish with thyme and serve immediately.

hot tip You can freeze leftovers of the soups in this chapter! Make sure you let the soup cool completely before storing in jars or containers. Thaw the soup in the fridge completely and then heat up to serve!

See Food Chowder

MAKES 6 servings
PREP TIME 45 minutes
COOK TIME 55 minutes

prep ahead

Tofu Bacon Crumbles (page 10)

ingredients

8 ounces shiitake mushrooms

8 ounces oyster mushrooms

3 tablespoons olive oil

1 teaspoon Old Bay seasoning

½ to 1 teaspoon sea salt

½ teaspoon ground pepper

1½ pounds small red potatoes, quartered (about 4 ½ cups quartered)

1 teaspoon fresh thyme leaves

1 cup raw cashews, soaked in hot water for 20 minutes

2 cups water

1 cup finely chopped onion (about 1 onion)

1 cup finely chopped carrot (about 1 large carrot)

1 cup finely chopped celery (about 2 stalks)

3 garlic cloves, minced

¼ teaspoon ground cayenne

¼ cup arrowroot flour or all-purpose flour

1 vegan chicken-flavored bouillon cube dissolved in 2 cups hot water, or 2 cups low-sodium vegetable stock

¾ cup dry white wine

1 cup unsweetened soy milk

4 hearts of palm, thinly sliced

1 cup frozen corn kernels

2 tablespoons finely chopped fresh dill

2 tablespoons finely chopped fresh flat-leaf parsley

Remember my story about the Crispy Crabless Cakes (page 53) and how John and I ate the most delicious ones at Lakeside (Wynn Hotel) in Las Vegas? Well the inspo for this See Food Chowder is essentially the same. This restaurant was a full seafood restaurant that had an equally great vegan menu with plant-based versions of things you didn't think you could ever find! And when I see food, more importantly anything that says the word vegan before it, I eat it! Then I recreate it, and now you lucky clams don't even need to go there 'cause you get this tasty rendition right here.

Preheat the oven to 425°F.

Leave most of the mushrooms whole, trim any woody stems from the shiitakes, and coarsely chop any particularly large shiitake or oyster mushrooms.

Toss the mushrooms on a baking sheet with 1 tablespoon of the olive oil, the Old Bay seasoning, and ¼ teaspoon each of the salt and pepper.

On another baking sheet, toss the potatoes with 1 tablespoon of the olive oil, the thyme, and the remaining ¼ teaspoon each salt and pepper.

Bake the mushrooms and potatoes at the same time. Place the mushrooms on the top rack; they'll take 13 to 15 minutes, depending on the size, until roasted and crispy in some spots. Place the potatoes on the middle rack; they'll take about 20 minutes until roasted and slightly crispy on the outside.

Meanwhile, drain and rinse the cashews and blend together with the water in a high-powered blender until very smooth.

In a large stockpot over medium heat, sauté the onion, carrot, and celery in the remaining 1 tablespoon olive oil for 4 to 5 minutes until softened and half cooked. Add the garlic and cayenne and sauté for 2 minutes. Lower the heat slightly to prevent burning.

Add the flour and stir constantly for 2 minutes. Once it's a little sticky and quite dry in the pot, add a bit of the stock to loosen and smooth out the mixture.

CONTINUED

2 tablespoons finely chopped nori seaweed

Tofu Bacon Crumbles, for garnish

Fresh dill sprigs or finely chopped fresh flat-leaf parsley, for garnish

Oyster crackers or vegan buttery crackers, for serving (optional)

Continue stirring while you add the wine. Bring to a simmer and cook for 2 minutes.

Constantly stir while slowly adding the soy milk and the cashew mixture and bring to a low simmer. Add the remaining stock and bring to a low simmer again. Add the mushrooms, potatoes, hearts of palm, corn, dill, parsley, and nori. Heat through for 10 to 15 minutes and serve immediately. Add salt to taste if you used low-sodium vegetable stock instead of bouillon.

Top with the bacon crumbles and garnish with the dill. Serve with oyster crackers or vegan buttery crackers, if desired.

cream of broccoli soup

MAKES 6 servings
PREP TIME 40 minutes
COOK TIME 30 minutes

ingredients

1 cup finely chopped onion
(about 1 onion)

¼ cup finely chopped shallot
(about 1 small shallot)

4 garlic cloves, minced

4 tablespoons vegan butter

½ teaspoon celery salt

½ teaspoon ground pepper,
plus more for seasoning

¼ teaspoon smoked paprika

¼ cup arrowroot flour or
all-purpose flour

3 cups unsweetened nondairy
milk

7 cups finely chopped broccoli
florets (about 3 crowns)

2 tablespoons chopped fresh dill

2 tablespoons chopped fresh
flat-leaf parsley

3 cups low-sodium vegetable
stock

Sea salt

2 cups vegan cheddar shreds,
for garnish (optional)

Smooth soup vs. chunky soup. Which reigns supreme? Well let's not debate each other too much because I'm on team chunk! There's nothing appealing about eating thick pureed soups that resemble baby food. I like chewing, so I keep my soups full of stuff to sink your teeth into! As such, I've made my cream of broccoli soup creamy and silky, but with broccoli florets dancing around the bowl so you still know what you're eating. I know I've pleased some of you with this decision, and as for the rest of you, you can blend the whole thing into sludge. I'll still love you!

In a large stockpot over medium heat, sauté the onion, shallot, and garlic in the vegan butter for 2 minutes.

Add the celery salt, pepper, and smoked paprika and sauté for another 2 minutes, lowering the heat slightly to prevent the garlic from burning.

Add the flour and stir constantly for 1 minute. Slowly add 2 cups of the nondairy milk while stirring constantly and bring to a simmer. Once the mixture is bubbling and thickened, add the broccoli and continue to stir constantly for 3 minutes. Once there is a smooth roux surrounding the broccoli florets, add the remaining 1 cup nondairy milk and continue to stir for 2 minutes. The broccoli should be slightly tender but still bright green. Add the dill and parsley and continue to cook for another minute. Add 1 cup of the stock and stir to combine.

Use a slotted spoon to remove about 1½ cups of the broccoli and other veg, straining the excess liquid as best you can, and reserve the veg in a bowl. Or if you're a baby, skip this step.

Blend the remaining soup in a blender until smooth or use an immersion blender in the pot. Add the soup back to the pot if you put it in a blender. Add the reserved broccoli and other veg along with the remaining 2 cups stock. Season with salt and ground pepper to taste. Bring to a low simmer and heat through for 10 minutes. The soup should still be fairly bright green as opposed to brown-green. Serve with cheddar shreds on top, if desired.

curried butternut squash soup

MAKES 6 servings
PREP TIME 50 minutes
COOK TIME 50 minutes

ingredients

1 (2-pound) butternut squash, peeled and cubed (about 4 cups cubed)

2 tablespoons olive oil

1¼ teaspoons sea salt

¾ teaspoon ground pepper

1 cup finely chopped onion (about 1 onion)

1 cup finely chopped carrot (about 1 large carrot)

1 cup finely chopped celery (about 2 stalks)

4 garlic cloves, minced

1 bay leaf

2 teaspoons fresh thyme leaves

1 teaspoon dried basil

1 teaspoon yellow curry powder

½ teaspoon ground fenugreek

½ teaspoon paprika

1 cup frozen corn kernels

1 cup diced vine tomatoes (about 2 tomatoes)

6 cups low-sodium vegetable stock

½ pound green beans, cut into 1-inch pieces (about 2 cups)

1 can (13.5 oz/400 ml) full-fat coconut milk

½ cup packed coarsely chopped fresh cilantro

1 tablespoon finely chopped fresh mint

3 cups packed baby spinach leaves

A spiced and satiating coconut curry broth mixed with fresh herbs and lots of veggies is my kind of soup for cold days or head colds! The butternut squash is obviously the fearless leader in this soup so I wanted to roast it before stirring it into the soup to give it an extra depth of flavor. Repurpose leftovers of this soup into a thicker curry served over rice or with rice noodles. Just add more full-fat coconut milk and maybe a little extra curry powder or paste to taste. Heat through and simmer until thick.

Preheat the oven to 425°F.

Toss the cubed butternut squash on a baking sheet with 1 tablespoon of the olive oil and ¼ teaspoon each of the salt and pepper. Roast for 20 to 25 minutes until tender and golden brown. Set aside.

When butternut squash has about 10 minutes remaining, begin making the soup in a stockpot. Over medium heat, sauté the onion, carrot, and celery in the remaining 1 tablespoon of olive oil for 4 minutes until just softened.

Add the garlic, bay leaf, thyme, basil, curry powder, fenugreek, paprika, remaining 1 teaspoon salt, and remaining ½ teaspoon pepper. Stir together and cook for 3 minutes until the garlic is cooked and fragrant. Lower the heat to prevent the garlic from burning.

Add the corn and tomatoes and cook for another 4 minutes, stirring occasionally.

Add the stock and bring to a low boil. Once the stock is bubbling, add the green beans and simmer for 5 minutes.

Stir in the coconut milk and bring to a low simmer. Once the liquid is bubbling, add the cilantro, mint, and butternut squash. Simmer for 5 minutes. Add the spinach and continue cooking for 5 to 10 minutes. Serve immediately!

hot tip I've used canned tomatoes to make this quick, but if you have a preference for homemade, try the fresh flavor of The Red Sauce (page 216). You could also add in veggie ground round after sautéing the zucchini and mushrooms for an even meatier version!

comforting lasagna soup

MAKES 6 to 8 servings
PREP TIME 30 minutes
COOK TIME 30 minutes

ingredients

1 cup finely chopped onion (about 1 onion)

2 tablespoons olive oil

3 garlic cloves, minced

1 bay leaf

1 teaspoon dried oregano

¼ teaspoon red pepper flakes

1 teaspoon sea salt

1 teaspoon ground pepper

3 cups diced zucchini (1 large zucchini)

4 cups sliced cremini mushrooms (about 10 ounces)

¼ cup tomato paste

2 tablespoons balsamic vinegar

2 teaspoons brown sugar

½ cup packed finely chopped fresh basil

½ cup packed fresh flat-leaf parsley, finely chopped

1 can (28 oz/794 g) crushed tomatoes

2 vegan beef-flavored bouillon cubes dissolved in 8 cups hot water, or 6 cups low-sodium vegetable stock and 2 cups water

12 lasagna noodles (not quick cooking)

6 cups packed baby spinach leaves

Vegan ricotta cheese or vegan mozzarella shreds, for garnish (optional)

Why lasagna soup you might be wondering? Well, sure, it's Pinterest worthy, but it's also a new way to savor more lasagna goodness! And lasagna might be the king of comfort food. Regular hot for foodies might know the best vegan lasagna recipe on the blog, so if you think I've gone too far with this, go ahead and stick to the straight and narrow. But if you love love love lasagna like I do, I promise you'll be obsessed with it as a soup.

In a large stockpot over medium heat, sauté the onion in the olive oil for 2 minutes until just softened.

Add the garlic, bay leaf, oregano, red pepper flakes, salt, and pepper and continue to sauté for 1 to 2 minutes, stirring constantly. Lower the heat to prevent the garlic from burning.

Add the zucchini and mushrooms and cook, stirring occasionally, for 6 minutes until most of the water from the vegetables is released and evaporates.

Add the tomato paste, vinegar, sugar, basil, and parsley and stir to combine. Cook for 2 minutes.

Add the tomatoes and stock. Break up the lasagna into smaller pieces and add to the pot. Bring to a boil and simmer for 10 to 12 minutes until the noodles are al dente. Stir occasionally to prevent the noodles from sticking and add the spinach in the last 2 minutes of cooking.

Serve immediately and garnish individual servings with dollops of vegan ricotta or top with vegan mozzarella shreds, if desired.

The noodles will absorb liquid if you have leftovers, so reheat the soup with extra water or stock to loosen the noodles, or enjoy the soup when it's thick like a stew.

stacked sandwiches

When I'm unsure of what I want to eat, which happens a lot, I always remember that my foodie soul will be become enlightened by a sandwich. Why? Because . . . bread. Bread gives me life. This chapter celebrates all the wonderful things you can stack between buns and bread. We're going to travel the world together with this sandwich selection, from New Orleans to Philly, Greece to Japan, England to Monte Cristo. Wait, that last one isn't a place?! But you'll definitely want to try the sandwich. To infinity and beyond!

oyster mushroom po' boy

MAKES 4 sandwiches
PREP TIME 45 minutes
COOK TIME 15 minutes

prep ahead

The Thousand Island (page 223)

fried oyster mushrooms

2 tablespoons ground flax

6 tablespoons water

1 cup unsweetened nondairy milk

¼ cup apple cider vinegar

2 tablespoons vegan oyster sauce or vegan Worcestershire

2 teaspoons garlic powder

2 teaspoons dried basil

1 teaspoon ground white or black pepper

8 ounces oyster mushrooms (16 to 20)

4 to 6 cups vegetable oil, for frying

breading

½ cup panko-style bread crumbs

¼ cup cornmeal

¼ cup all-purpose flour

1 teaspoon sea salt

1 teaspoon ground cayenne

1 teaspoon garlic powder

1 teaspoon dried basil

½ teaspoon smoked paprika

½ teaspoon ground pepper

sandwiches

4 hoagie or kaiser-style rolls

The Thousand Island

2½ cups finely chopped romaine lettuce

3 vine tomatoes, thinly sliced

3 dill pickles, sliced into rounds

This is my tribute to Guy Fieri, the host of Diners, Drive-Ins, and Dives! I equally loathe and am enamored with his show on the Food Network, as well as with Guy himself. On one hand I want nothing to do with him and what his food stands for, yet on the other hand I want to BE him. I just would never be caught dead in a flame shirt! So I wanted to make a version of a po' boy sandwich because there's always one of these on Triple D. Shrimp, lobster, crab, oysters, you name it, Guy finds it, and they're all over America, not just in New Orleans (where the sandwich originated). So sink your big mouth into this sammich and tell me being vegan ain't the greatest! Welcome to flavor town.

To prepare the mushrooms, mix together the ground flax and water in a bowl and let sit for 10 minutes to thicken.

In another bowl, mix together the nondairy milk, vinegar, oyster sauce, garlic powder, basil, and pepper. Add the flax mixture and pour the marinade over the mushrooms in a large zipper bag, making sure they are well submerged. Refrigerate for at least 20 minutes. Or you can leave it overnight.

Heat the oil in a heavy-bottomed pot to a temperature of 365°F to 375°F on a deep-frying thermometer. The oil should be heated to the right temperature just as you're about to bread the mushrooms.

To make the breading, mix together all the ingredients in a bowl.

Remove a few mushrooms from the marinade and place directly in the breading, coating evenly on all sides using your hands. Place each piece in the hot oil and fry for 2 to 3 minutes.

Place fried mushrooms on paper towels to absorb excess oil. Continue to bread the mushrooms and fry in small batches.

To assemble the sandwiches, cut the rolls in half and toast, if desired. Spread some Thousand Island on the inside of each roll. Layer the romaine lettuce, tomato slices, pickles, and fried mushrooms on one half of each roll. Add more of Thousand Island, if desired. Serve immediately while the oyster mushrooms are still warm.

Reheat leftover fried mushrooms in a 425°F oven for 10 to 12 minutes until crispy.

hot tip Try this seitan as a Rueben or corned beef-style sandwich with spicy mustard and sauerkraut on rye bread!

saved by seitan

MAKES 1 large loaf (enough for both sandwich recipes)
PREP TIME 40 minutes, plus curing seitan overnight
COOK TIME 90 minutes

ingredients

- 3 cups vital wheat gluten
- ¼ cup nutritional yeast
- 2 teaspoons onion powder
- 1 teaspoon sea salt
- 1 teaspoon celery salt
- 1 teaspoon smoked paprika
- 1 teaspoon garlic powder
- 1 teaspoon dried thyme
- 1 teaspoon dried oregano
- 1 teaspoon dried basil
- 1 teaspoon ground mustard
- 1 teaspoon ground pepper
- 2 vegan beef-flavored bouillon cubes dissolved in 3 cups hot water, or 3 cups low-sodium vegetable stock
- ¼ cup vegetable oil
- 2 tablespoons low-sodium tamari or soy sauce
- 2 tablespoons apple cider vinegar
- 1 tablespoon tomato paste

I've been saved by seitan! Or maybe I just saved myself because this is the perfect seitan "beef" for the Philly Cheesesteak (page 96) and Gyro Wrap (page 99). But by all means, get dirty with it and experiment. There are so many ways to make seitan or "wheat meat" with slightly different textures that work for whatever you're dreaming of making. I achieved a firm, chewy texture here that works when sliced very thin to mimic shaved beef or lamb. So if you're a vegan who craves the carnivorous meals you used to eat, I don't judge or blame you, and I've gotcha covered!

Preheat the oven to 350°F.

In a large bowl, combine the wheat gluten with the nutritional yeast, spices, and herbs.

In another bowl, mix together the stock, vegetable oil, tamari, vinegar, and tomato paste until well combined.

Pour the stock mixture into the wheat gluten mixture and stir to combine.

The mixture should be very moist, but still able to be handled as one large piece. It should not be sticking to your hands, but should be quite slippery. You will feel the elasticity of the gluten binding it together into a blob. Place the dough on a clean work surface and knead, pulling and stretching it and folding it over itself a few times. Finally, press it together to form large log shape approximately 10 inches long and 5 inches in diameter.

Wrap the log tightly in a large piece of heavy-duty aluminum foil. You may need to use 2 sheets to make it completely secure. There should be no exposed gaps. Tighten and twist the ends of the foil.

Place the log on a baking sheet and bake for 90 minutes. It should feel very firm when you take it out of the oven. Allow the log to cool at room temperature. Store in the fridge overnight before using it for sandwiches.

The seitan is best sliced very thin with a sharp knife or shaved using a mandolin.

Store the seitan in the fridge and consume within 10 days. Or it can be portioned and wrapped to freeze for longer storage, up to 2 months. Thaw completely before slicing and using in sandwiches.

philly cheesesteak

MAKES 6 sandwiches
PREP TIME 25 minutes
COOK TIME 20 minutes

prep ahead

Saved by Seitan (page 95)

The Nacho Cheese (page 205)

ingredients

2 cups thinly sliced onions
(about 2 onions)

2 cups thinly sliced green bell
peppers (about 2 peppers)

2 tablespoons vegetable oil

½ Saved by Seitan loaf, thinly
sliced or shaved

2 tablespoons vegan
Worcestershire

2 tablespoons water

Sea salt and ground pepper

6 hoagie-style buns

6 tablespoons vegan butter

The Nacho Cheese, warmed

In west Philadelphia, born and raised, on the playground was where I spent most of my days . . . nope not true. But you knew that. Am I the only one whose reference for Philly cheesesteaks comes from watching the Fresh Prince drool and reminisce over them in that greasy paper bag? You can find this montage on YouTube, FYI. It always made my mouth water, but I've never eaten one with real steak. Though, I have had my fair share of vegan Philly cheesesteaks and I've really gotta give it up for my own creation. I'm sure you'll agree after just one big bite!

In a large cast-iron skillet or frying pan over medium heat, sauté the onions and bell peppers with the vegetable oil for 10 to 12 minutes until soft and cooked through. Add the sliced seitan and brown for 3 to 4 minutes.

Combine the Worcestershire and water together in a small bowl. Pour over the vegetables and seitan and toss to coat everything in the sauce. Continue cooking for 3 minutes. Add salt and pepper to taste.

Meanwhile, cut the hoagie buns in half. Toast and butter the buns. Spread the warm cheese on the inside of both halves of each bun. Top with a generous portion of the seitan mixture. Drizzle with more cheese and serve immediately.

gyro wrap

MAKES 6 wraps
PREP TIME 35 minutes
COOK TIME 6 minutes

prep ahead

Saved by Seitan (page 95)

The Creamy Cucumber
(page 223)

ingredients

2 teaspoons vegetable oil

½ Saved by Seitan loaf, thinly
sliced or shaved

½ teaspoon dried oregano

Sea salt and ground pepper

6 large pita breads

The Creamy Cucumber

6 cups packed baby spinach
or lettuce of your choice

3 cups packed alfalfa sprouts
(optional)

2 vine tomatoes, sliced

1 cup thinly sliced red onion
(about 1 onion)

1 cup thinly sliced English
cucumber (about 1 cucumber)

Make Saved by Seitan (page 95) and you're in sandwich heaven for a few days. There's enough wheat meat to make both the Philly Cheesesteak (page 96) and this Greek-inspired gyro wrap! I have to say, gyro or shawarma meat has to be one of the most unappetizing-looking things you could eat as an omnivore. I wouldn't touch that stuff with a 10-foot skewer! Get it? But this super-stuffed wrap has all the elements you're looking for, is far healthier, and The Creamy Cucumber (page 223) really ties it all together. You can even add the tofu feta from My Big Fat Greek Potato Salad (page 67) for an extra kick.

Heat the vegetable oil in a large cast-iron skillet or frying pan over medium heat. Add the seitan and oregano and season with salt and ground pepper. Toss together and brown for 5 to 6 minutes.

Meanwhile, warm the pitas in the oven or a toaster, if desired.

Spread some creamy cucumber dressing on each pita. Place the spinach, sprouts, tomato slices, onion slices, cucumber slices, and a generous portion of seitan on top. Drizzle more creamy cucumber on top and roll tightly. Wrap one end of the roll in aluminum foil or parchment paper to contain the contents and serve immediately! You could also stuff everything inside the pita and make pockets, but I find they break all the time.

filet-o-tempeh sandwich

MAKES 4 sandwiches
PREP TIME 35 minutes,
plus 30 minutes to 6 hours
for marinating
COOK TIME 8 minutes

prep ahead

The Tartar Sauce (page 207)

beer-battered tempeh

1 brick (8 oz/225 g) tempeh

⅓ cup water

⅓ cup white wine vinegar

2 tablespoons freshly squeezed
lemon juice

3 teaspoons Old Bay seasoning

2 teaspoons sea salt

1½ teaspoons ground pepper

4 to 6 cups vegetable oil,
for frying

1 cup all-purpose flour

2 tablespoons baking powder

½ teaspoon paprika

1 cup cold vegan-friendly lager
or ale

sandwiches

4 whole wheat, sprouted,
or sesame seed buns

The Tartar Sauce

2 cups packed sunflower
sprouts or shredded iceberg
lettuce

1 avocado, pitted, peeled,
quartered, and sliced

Think of this as your ocean-friendly filet-o-fish sandwich. Because we all know the only sustainable seafood is no seafood at all. If you've ever become enamoured with a Planet Earth documentary, you sure as hell have realized how brilliant fish are. I don't want to eat something smarter than me. Anyway, back to the food at hand. Tempeh is one of my favorite plant proteins, but I know a lot of people cringe at it. Me thinks, they had undercooked and underseasoned versions. This tempeh "fish" was a John creation back in the day, and we thought it needed to become an epic sandwich. So this may be your intro into the world of tempeh, but it's a good one. If you want to swap club soda for the beer, go ahead, but you need the fizz to make the batter nice and fluffy. I love to serve this sandwich with salt and vinegar chips and an icy cold beer!

To marinate the tempeh, slice the brick of tempeh in half and slice each half lengthwise so you have 4 thin fillets.

Combine the water, vinegar, lemon juice, 2 teaspoons of the Old Bay, and 1 teaspoon each salt and pepper in a shallow dish and submerge the tempeh fillets in the marinade. Refrigerate for at least 30 minutes or up to 6 hours. Do not leave them longer than that or they may be too soft to handle without breaking.

When you are ready to fry the tempeh, add vegetable oil to a heavy-bottomed pot or deep fryer and heat to 350°F or as high as 360°F on a deep-frying thermometer.

To make the batter, put ¼ cup of the flour in a bowl. In another bowl, combine the remaining ¾ cup flour, remaining teaspoon salt, remaining teaspoon Old Bay seasoning, and remaining ½ teaspoon ground pepper with the baking powder and paprika. Leave out the beer until the oil is hot enough to fry.

Take each tempeh fillet from the marinade and dredge through the flour, getting all sides well coated.

When you're ready to fry, gently stir the beer into the flour and spice mixture. Don't stir too much, as you want air in the batter.

CONTINUED

Coat a fillet in the beer batter and put it directly into the hot oil. You'll probably need to do 1 fillet at a time so you don't overcrowd the pot. Cook for 2 minutes, flipping the fillet after 1 minute, until golden brown.

Using a slotted frying spoon, remove the fried tempeh fillet to a wire rack set over a baking sheet. This will help keep the fillets crispy while you continue frying. Laying them on paper towels could make the fillets soggy. Make sure the oil is still between 350°F and 365°F before frying another fillet.

To assemble the sandwiches, cut the buns in half and toast, if desired. Spread some tartar sauce on the bottom half of each bun, then add the sprouts, a fillet, avocado slices, and more tartar sauce on top.

These are best consumed right after frying, but leftover fried fillets can be refrigerated and consumed within 4 to 5 days. Warm the fillets over medium-high heat in a pan or in a preheated 375°F oven. However, they might not get as crispy as when you first fried them.

buffalo cauliflower sandwich

MAKES 4 sandwiches
PREP TIME 30 minutes
COOK TIME 50 minutes

prep ahead

The Classic Ranch (page 223)

breaded buffalo cauliflower

2 heads cauliflower

1½ cups all-purpose flour or gluten-free rice flour

4 teaspoons garlic powder

4 teaspoons onion powder

2 teaspoons ground cumin

2 teaspoons paprika

½ teaspoon sea salt

½ teaspoon ground pepper

¾ cup unsweetened nondairy milk

¾ cup water

3 cups panko-style bread crumbs or gluten-free bread crumbs

¼ cup vegan butter

1½ cups buffalo-style hot sauce

sandwiches

4 kaiser-style rolls

The Classic Ranch

1 cup thinly sliced red onion (about 1 onion) or Pickled Red Onions (page 107)

2 cups shredded or finely chopped iceberg or leaf lettuce

2 tomatoes, thinly sliced

4 dill pickles

It's our claim to fame . . . buffalo cauliflower. This recipe is the most visited page on the blog and the most watched YouTube video. Newcomers, feast your eyes on the buffalo cauliflower sandwich! You diehards will notice and recognize the revamp on the breading. I've added panko-style bread crumbs 'cause it makes the cauliflower crispy and crunchy as hell. Not the kind of crunch that'll tear up the roof of your mouth, but the kind of crunch that'll definitely make you relapse and forget that you're biting into a piece of cauliflower. It makes a heck of a good replacement for chicken in this spicy stacked monster of a sandwich!

Preheat the oven to 450°F. Line a baking sheet with parchment paper. In this case, parchment paper is absolutely necessary, or the cauliflower and batter will stick to the sheet.

To prepare the cauliflower, remove the leafy parts, being careful not to cut off any florets. Slice each head in half from the top. From the inside of each half, cut a slice ¾ inch to 1 inch thick. You now have 4 large cauliflower cross-sections or steaks. You can reserve the remaining florets to make buffalo bites using the same batter and method or the Southern Fried Cauliflower (page 46), or you can roast them up for another meal.

Mix the flour, garlic powder, onion powder, cumin, paprika, salt, pepper, nondairy milk, and water together in a bowl until well combined. The amount of liquid or flour may need to be increased if you replace the all-purpose flour with gluten-free flour. It should be thick enough that it doesn't pool too much around the steak.

Transfer the batter to a wide, shallow dish that will fit your cauliflower steaks. Place the bread crumbs in another dish or large bowl. Immerse each steak in the batter, using one hand to coat all the crevices and letting just a bit of the excess drip back into the dish.

Coat all sides of the steaks in the bread crumbs. Place the breaded cauliflower steaks on the baking sheet.

CONTINUED

Bake for 25 minutes, until crispy, flipping the steaks halfway through the bake time. If you go to flip the steaks and the batter feels stuck, it needs to bake longer on that side.

Just before the cauliflower finishes baking, melt the vegan butter and whisk it into the hot sauce in a shallow dish.

Remove the cauliflower from the oven. You may want to let the steaks cool slightly so you can handle them. You may need to replace the parchment paper with a new sheet if it's really soaked through or burned quite a bit.

Coat the breaded cauliflower steaks evenly on all sides in the buffalo sauce. Reserve the excess sauce to baste the cauliflower before serving. Bake again for 25 minutes, flipping the steaks halfway through the bake time.

To assemble the sandwiches, just before the cauliflower is done baking, cut the rolls in half and toast, if desired. Spread a generous amount of ranch dressing on the cut sides of each roll. Place a buffalo cauliflower steak on the bottom half. Add the red onion slices, lettuce, tomato slices, and then the top half of the roll. Serve with a pickle or slice the pickles and add to the sandwich.

hot tip You can slice leftover buffalo cauliflower steaks into breaded strips and make a salad with greens and veggies like tomatoes, cucumbers, and red onion. Then drown it in ranch dressing. It's outstanding! You can also use half buffalo-style hot sauce and half BBQ sauce for a milder version of this sandwich.

hot tip The best place to look for cans of jackfruit is in Asian supermarkets or Chinatown. You might notice that can sizes vary from 14 ounces to 20 ounces, but it's essentially the same amount of usable fruit once drained, so our recipe should work out fine with the brands readily available. If the fruit doesn't feel too soft and can't be shredded by hand easily right out of the can, you might have fruit that's nearly raw. It will need to be boiled for 20 to 30 minutes before cooking the way I've instructed to get it tender. Not all cans are created equal!

bbq jackfruit sandwich

MAKES 4 sandwiches
PREP TIME 50 minutes, plus
2 hours or overnight for pickling
COOK TIME 10 minutes

prep ahead

The Jalapeño-Lime Aioli
(page 227)

The BBQ Sauce (page 209)

pickled red onions

1 large red onion

½ cup white wine vinegar

1 tablespoon sea salt

1 tablespoon granulated sugar

½ to 1 cup water

slaw

3 cups shredded or finely
chopped napa cabbage

1 cup packed baby spinach,
finely chopped

2 green onions, white and green
parts, finely chopped

2 tablespoons finely chopped
fresh mint

2 tablespoons finely chopped
fresh cilantro

½ cup The Jalapeño-Lime Aioli

Ground pepper

bbq jackfruit

2 cans young jackfruit in water
or brine (not syrup, see hot tip)

2 teaspoons vegetable oil

1 cup The BBQ Sauce

Sea salt and ground pepper

sandwiches

4 kaiser or ciabatta-style rolls

¼ cup The Jalapeño-Lime Aioli

A fruit that looks like meat? No you haven't fallen into an alternate universe! If you've never seen or heard of jackfruit, you'll be truly fooled and pleasantly surprised by this sandwich. While you could skip the pickled onions, they really add a nice element to the sandwich. You can also make this recipe even easier by using your favorite store-bought BBQ sauce rather than our homemade version. I won't negotiate on that slaw though. The aroma from the fresh herbs and mix of textures when the cool creamy slaw meshes with the sweet and smoky jackfruit is perfect. If you're not drooling right now, you might want to check your pulse!

To make the pickled onions, thinly slice the onion with a mandolin. If you don't have one, use a sharp knife and slice the onions as thin as you can so you can see the knife through the slices. Combine the vinegar, sea salt, and sugar in a glass bowl or large jar. Add the onions and fill with water to submerge and cover all the onions. Refrigerate for as little as 2 hours, but overnight is best if you can prep ahead. Consume within 2 weeks.

To prepare the slaw, combine all the ingredients together in a bowl. Refrigerate while you prepare the jackfruit.

To prepare the jackfruit, drain the jackfruit and rinse well. Squeeze out the excess liquid from the fruit through a sieve if the fruit seems excessively watery. Pat dry with paper towels.

Heat a pan over medium heat with the vegetable oil and add the jackfruit, pulling it with your hands or breaking it up with a fork into shreds. Break up small bulbs or remove them if you prefer. Sauté for 5 to 6 minutes until lightly browned. Add the BBQ sauce. Turn the heat to medium-low and cook for another 4 to 5 minutes. Add salt and pepper to taste, if necessary.

To assemble the sandwiches, cut the rolls in half and toast, if desired. Spread a generous amount of aioli on both cut sides of each roll. Add slaw to the bottom half, then a generous amount of jackfruit, and top with pickled onions and the top half of the roll. Serve immediately while still warm.

Keep leftover jackfruit refrigerated for up to 5 days. Reheat the jackfruit in a microwave or sauté it in a pan for a few minutes until heated through.

monte cristo

MAKES 4 sandwiches
PREP TIME 20 minutes
COOK TIME 35 minutes

prep ahead

Tofu Bacon Slices (page 10)

ingredients

1 cup unsweetened nondairy milk

⅓ cup chickpea flour

3 tablespoons nutritional yeast

2 tablespoons maple syrup

½ teaspoon sea salt

8 slices sourdough bread

4 tablespoons vegan butter, for frying

2 tablespoons Dijon mustard

2 tablespoons vegan mayonnaise

12 vegan provolone or cheddar cheese slices

Tofu Bacon Slices

1 to 2 teaspoons confectioners' sugar (optional)

¼ cup maple syrup or raspberry jam, for serving

This sandwich is from John's childhood memory bank. I didn't even know what a Monte Cristo was until I met him, and he told me all the strange tales of what he ate growing up on his family's farm. We had much to learn from each other's history with food, and it's the dichotomy between us that makes hot for food recipes so great! So if you don't know what a Monte Cristo is, it's basically a French toast grilled cheese sandwich traditionally made with ham, turkey, and cheese in the middle. Oh, and powdered sugar on top . . . because, America. Sounds kinda gross and kinda awesome all at the same time right? But one thing's for sure . . . this sandwich is a surefire hangover cure!

Combine the nondairy milk, chickpea flour, nutritional yeast, maple syrup, and salt in a wide, shallow dish. Place 2 slices of bread into the batter and allow the slices to sit in the batter for 1 to 2 minutes. Depending on the thickness and type of bread you're using, you might want to soak for more or less time. The slices should be well coated on both sides but not overly soggy.

Meanwhile, heat a large nonstick skillet over medium heat with 1 tablespoon of the vegan butter.

Place 2 battered slices of the bread in the pan and cook on one side for approximately 3 minutes. Flip and put Dijon mustard on 1 slice and vegan mayonnaise on the other. Use 3 slices of cheese per sandwich and divide between the 2 pieces of bread. Top 1 bread slice with a few pieces of the bacon slices. Continue to cook for 3 minutes, then put the two halves together to assemble the sandwich, lower the heat, and cover the pan with a lid. The cheese should melt in another 2 minutes, but the heat should be low enough that the bread won't burn.

Repeat with the remaining sandwiches. Adjust the heat as you go and continue frying each sandwich, adding 1 tablespoon of the vegan butter to the pan for each one.

Top the finished sandwiches with confectioners' sugar, if desired, and serve with maple syrup for dipping.

the ramen burger

MAKES 4 sandwiches
PREP TIME 20 minutes
COOK TIME 35 minutes

prep ahead

The Thousand Island (page 223)
or The Spicy Sriracha Aioli
(page 227)

The BBQ Sauce
(page 209), optional

sandwiches

1 tablespoon oil

4 vegan burger patties, or
8 patties for a double decker

½ cup The BBQ Sauce

4 vegan cheddar cheese slices

½ cup The Thousand Island
or The Spicy Sriracha Aioli

2 cups shredded lettuce

1 tomato, sliced thick

ramen patties

2 vegan onion or other bouillon
cubes dissolved in 3 cups water,
or 3 cups low-sodium vegetable
stock

4 (3 oz/100 g) packs instant
ramen noodles (vegan-friendly)

2 tablespoons vegetable oil,
for frying

I ain't frontin'! This idea belongs right up there with a leaked Kardashian nude, a Bieber breakup, or anything Kanye tweets. It's a tad stunty, but I had to, 'cause it's friggin' delicious! The ramen burger would fit in at a birthday bash, kegger, or potluck, or maybe one of those Friday nights when you just want to impress yourself and your dog. This sandwich is a bit of a messy one, and you will not look good eating it. But I dare you to take a walk where the wild things are, and if you make this please send noods to @hotforfood.

To make the sandwiches, heat the oil in a skillet over medium heat and cook the burger patties for about 3 minutes on each side or until lightly charred. Then coat one cooked side with the BBQ sauce, flip, coat the other side, and cook for another 3 minutes. Flip, place a cheddar slice on top, and cook for 3 more minutes. Lower the heat or turn off the heat and cover the pan to keep the patties warm and continue melting the cheese.

Meanwhile, prepare the ramen patties. Bring the stock to a boil. Add the noodles and cook for 3 minutes. You could also use the instant ramen flavor packet instead of bouillon or stock. Drain the ramen but do not rinse.

Heat a nonstick pan over medium heat and add a coating of vegetable oil. Lightly coat 1 or 2 ring molds, each 2½ inches in diameter, with vegetable oil. Place the ring molds in the pan. Fill each ring with ramen noodles to just below the top edge. Oil a spatula or spoon and use it to press and pack the noodles firmly in the rings while you cook them for 2 to 3 minutes. Flip the ring and again press the ramen patties down to cook the other side for approximately 2 minutes. Reduce the heat to medium-low as the pan gets hotter. Remove the cooked ramen patties to a wire rack and gently remove the rings. You might need to trim any stuck noodles, but don't pull them or the patty will unravel. Continue this process until you have 8 ramen patties. As long as the rings and the pan are oiled, there shouldn't be much unraveling.

To assemble the sandwiches, coat one side of each ramen patty with Thousand Island. Place a handful of lettuce on top, then add a burger patty with melted cheese, tomato, and another drizzle of BBQ sauce, and top with a ramen patty.

oodles of noodles

I have a confession: if I could live on any of my recipes, it would definitely be a pasta dish. Talk about comfort! All pillowy, soft, silky, and creamy. Yeah, that's luxury! I wanted to triple this chapter but I had to control myself. My pasta cravings are real and frequent. So can we just stop it with the pasta shaming? When you want pasta, eat pasta. Cause YOLO! Anyone who attempts to talk you out of eating pasta isn't a real friend. Rant over. In this chapter you can work your way from novice to expert, starting with some of the über-simple ideas like the Spicy Peanut Noodles (page 121) or Green Pea Pesto Linguine (page 122), and when you finally master The Best Vegan Ramen (page 132), you basically win at life.

mushroom fettuccine alfredo

MAKES 4 to 6 servings
PREP TIME 30 minutes
COOK TIME 25 minutes

prep ahead

The Parm (page 207)

ingredients

1 pound fettuccine

1½ cups raw cashews, soaked in hot water for 20 minutes

1 cup water

1 teaspoon apple cider vinegar

1 tablespoon freshly squeezed lemon juice, plus 1 to 2 teaspoons (optional)

1 cup finely chopped onion (about 1 onion)

2 tablespoons olive oil

2 large portobello mushrooms, thinly sliced

4 cups thinly sliced cremini mushrooms (about 10 ounces)

4 garlic cloves, minced

½ to 1 teaspoon sea salt, plus more for seasoning

½ teaspoon ground pepper, plus more for seasoning

½ cup dry white wine or low-sodium vegetable stock

2 tablespoons finely chopped fresh basil

1 teaspoon dried parsley

4 cups packed baby spinach

1 cup low-sodium vegetable stock

¼ cup The Parm

Here's a classic no one ever thinks could possibly be re-created without butter and heavy cream. But it can be done, and this one won't weigh you down for days with loads of dairy. So say hello to the creamiest-ever vegan fettuccine Alfredo! If you're a mushroom hater, I don't understand your life, but you can leave them out. The wine, however, is nonnegotiable. Okay, if you have to omit it I've got you covered below. Oh, and if you're allergic to nuts, just replace the cashews with the same measurement of soft tofu and use ½ cup water when blending. Okay, no more excuses . . . get cooking!

Bring a large pot of salted water to a boil. Cook the pasta until al dente. Drain, but do not rinse.

Meanwhile, drain and rinse the cashews and add to a high-powered blender along with the water, vinegar, and 1 tablespoon lemon juice. Blend until very smooth.

In a large pan over medium heat, sauté the onion in the olive oil for 2 minutes until just softened. Add the mushrooms and cook for 4 minutes. When mushrooms are half cooked and start to release some moisture, stir in the garlic, salt, and pepper and cook for 3 to 4 minutes.

Once mushrooms have shrunk and released most of their moisture, add the white wine. Add the 1 to 2 teaspoons lemon juice if using stock in place of the wine. Simmer for 7 minutes until most of the liquid has reduced. Reduce heat to medium-low, stir in the basil and parsley, and cook for another minute. Stir in the cashew cream and spinach, and slowly stir in the stock. Cook for about 4 minutes until the spinach is wilted and soft but still bright green.

Add the pasta to the pan and toss to combine everything well. Cook for 3 minutes.

Serve immediately and add The Parm on top and ground pepper and salt to taste. If reheating leftovers, heat in a pan and add small amounts of vegetable stock while tossing the pasta to thin out the sauce. Refrigerate any leftovers and consume within 5 days.

cold cucumber—chile noodles

MAKES 4 to 6 servings
PREP TIME 20 minutes
COOK TIME 6-8 minutes

ingredients

- 1 pound thick flat rice noodles
- 2 English cucumbers
- 2 green onions, white and green parts, finely sliced diagonally
- 2 tablespoons toasted sesame oil
- 2 tablespoons sesame seeds
- ¼ to ½ teaspoon sea salt
- 4 tablespoons chile oil

I tend to add megaflavor to everything I cook, but in this dish I embrace the minimalist trend and really like the simplicity of green onions with spice, sesame, salt, and refreshing crunchy cucumber. It was inspired by something I ate a couple of years ago at Xi'an Famous Foods in Brooklyn. A friend claimed this menu item, known as A-1, was her favorite thing ever, which I mistook for hyperbole. But I was curious. Well, after ordering it and taking one bite, I was in love and certainly wasn't prepared for a long-distance relationship with this noodle dish so I made my own version!

Bring a large pot of salted water to a boil. If your rice noodles already contain salt, do not add salt to the water. Cook the noodles until al dente, approximately 6 minutes.

Meanwhile, cut the cucumber into ribbons using a vegetable peeler or slice very thin using a mandolin.

Drain the noodles, rinse under cool water, and place in a large bowl. Toss with the cucumber ribbons, green onions, sesame oil, sesame seeds (reserving 1 teaspoon for garnish), and ¼ teaspoon of the salt (more to taste, if necessary). Divide among serving plates.

Drizzle each portion with 1 tablespoon of the chile oil (or use more sesame oil if you don't want spice) and garnish with the remaining sesame seeds. You can also toss the noodles in only the sesame oil, salt, and sesame seeds, leaving the cucumber ribbons and green onions to place on top of the noodles in each serving. I think this looks prettier!

If you have leftovers, soften the noodles by heating them with a bit of water in a covered pan or heat in a microwave. Drain any excess water before serving.

creamy rosé penne

MAKES 4 to 6 servings
COOK TIME 20 minutes

prep ahead

The Rosé Sauce (page 216)

The Parm (page 207)

ingredients

1 pound penne

5 to 6 cups The Rosé Sauce

½ cup The Parm

1 to 2 teaspoons red pepper flakes (optional)

Sea salt and ground pepper

As elaborate and varied as noodle dishes can be, sometimes you just want to channel your inner college kid and eat pasta with tomato sauce. Our rich rosé sauce on penne is a splendid solution for easy weeknight dinners. But if you're looking to beef this up, you could add steamed vegetables, sautéed veggie ground round, or Tofu Bacon Crumbles (page 10).

Bring a pot of salted water to a boil and cook the pasta until al dente. Drain but don't rinse.

Add the pasta back to the pot you cooked it in and place over low heat. Add 4 to 5 cups of the sauce (or more if desired). Stir to coat evenly and heat through for 3 to 4 minutes. Stir in ¼ cup of The Parm.

Top each serving with a bit more sauce, if desired, as well as more of The Parm, the red pepper flakes, and salt and pepper to taste.

spicy peanut noodles

MAKES 4 to 6 servings
PREP TIME 30 minutes
COOK TIME 15 minutes

prep ahead

The Spicy Peanut Sauce
(page 215)

ingredients

1 pound linguine, spaghetti, or flat rice noodles

2 tablespoons vegetable oil

1 cup thinly sliced onion (about 1 onion)

3 green onions, white and green parts, finely sliced diagonally

2 garlic cloves, minced

1 or more red Thai chiles, seeds removed and finely chopped

1 teaspoon minced fresh ginger

1 cup thinly sliced red bell pepper (about 1 pepper)

1 broccoli crown, cut into florets

1 cup snow peas

1 cup The Spicy Peanut Sauce

½ to 1 teaspoon sea salt

½ cup packed fresh cilantro leaves, coarsely chopped, for garnish

⅓ cup salted roasted peanuts, coarsely chopped, for garnish

1 lime, cut into wedges, for garnish

You know those lazy nights when you want to order takeout? For me, I usually crave some kind of Thai noodles or curry. But they're seriously never as good as I imagine they're going to be when I ravenously place the order and it takes 45 minutes to show up on my doorstep! I know, first world problems. But the moral of the story is if you want something done right, you have to do it yourself. These noodles are just what you're craving, and you'll be slurping them up in 30 minutes or less, no tip required.

Bring a pot of salted water to a boil and cook the noodles until al dente. Drain, but do not rinse.

Meanwhile, heat a large frying pan or wok with the vegetable oil over medium-high heat. Once the pan is hot, add the sliced onion and the white parts of the green onion (reserving the green parts for garnish) and sauté for 2 to 3 minutes until just softened.

Add the garlic, chiles to taste, and ginger and sauté for 2 minutes until soft and fragrant. Lower the heat slightly if the mixture starts to burn.

Add the bell pepper and sauté for 2 minutes until just softened.

Add the broccoli florets and snow peas and sauté for 6 minutes until about half cooked, but still bright green.

Add half of the peanut sauce and toss to coat well. Toss in the cooked noodles and the remaining sauce. Lower the heat, toss to coat thoroughly, and heat through. At this point, you can add ½ to 1 teaspoon of the salt to taste.

Serve immediately, as the noodles start to get slightly sticky the longer they sit. Garnish with the cilantro, peanuts, remaining green onions, and lime wedges.

Leftovers can be reheated in a pan over medium heat with a bit of water, or a combination of coconut milk and water, to loosen the noodles and sauce. Consume leftovers within 5 to 7 days.

green pea pesto linguine

MAKES 4 servings
PREP TIME 20 minutes
COOK TIME 12 minutes

prep ahead

The Parm (page 207)

ingredients

1 pound linguine

2 cups fresh or frozen peas

1 teaspoon sea salt

2 cups packed fresh basil leaves, plus more for garnish

2 garlic cloves

½ cup The Parm

¼ cup freshly squeezed lemon juice

¼ cup olive oil

Ground pepper

I love this pesto! It's made in 10 minutes, hides my vegetables in a pile of cheesy garlicky stuff, and can even become a dip for crackers and veggies. This is my ultimate reduce, reuse, and recycle food! But as multipurpose as this pesto is, it's still most epic served on pasta, and it certainly ain't picky about the shape. I just thought linguine needed to join the party for this one. Feel free to use whatever you have lying around.

Bring a large pot of salted water to a boil. Cook the linguine until al dente and add 1 cup of the peas to the water in the last minute of cooking. Drain, but do not rinse.

While the pasta is cooking, combine the remaining 1 cup peas (thawed and drained of excess water, if frozen), salt, 2 cups basil leaves, garlic, ¼ cup of The Parm, lemon juice, and olive oil in a food processor until well combined and smooth but textured.

Place the drained pasta and peas back in the pot while it's still warm. Add three-fourths of the pesto and toss to combine well.

Serve the pasta with an extra dollop of pesto on top. Garnish with the remainder of The Parm, ground pepper to taste, and basil leaves.

eggplant parm & spaghetti

MAKES 4 servings
PREP TIME 50 minutes
COOK TIME 30-40 minutes

prep ahead

The Red Sauce (page 216)

The Parm (page 207)

cheese sauce

1 large eggplant

1½ teaspoons sea salt

1 teaspoon plus
1 tablespoon olive oil

¾ cup unsweetened nondairy milk

1 tablespoon tapioca flour

1 teaspoon nutritional yeast

½ teaspoon garlic powder

¼ teaspoon onion powder

¼ teaspoon ground white pepper

2 teaspoons freshly squeezed lemon juice

saucy spaghetti

1 pound spaghetti

5 to 6 cups The Red Sauce

fried eggplant

2 cups vegetable oil, for frying

1 cup bread crumbs

½ cup The Parm

1 teaspoon garlic powder

1 teaspoon dried oregano

1 teaspoon dried basil

¼ teaspoon sea salt

¼ teaspoon ground pepper

½ cup all-purpose flour

½ cup unsweetened nondairy milk

All plants are created equal . . . except the eggplant. The eggplant is like that certain someone who hasn't updated his or her hairdo since the '80s. Out of touch! And eggplant parm is the dish that EVERYONE thinks you eat as a vegetarian/vegan. Every time someone at a dinner says, "Don't worry I made something for you," it's either quinoa or eggplant parm. Clearly I've been the guest at these dinner parties far too many times, which is why you won't find quinoa anywhere near these pages and why my eggplant parm has been given a serious makeover. If you deep-fry anything, smother it in homemade tomato sauce, and serve it with pasta, well, now it's palatable. This dish has a new 'do and it's ready for date night!

To make the cheese sauce, trim the stem and a small part of the base of the eggplant. Peel the entire eggplant, if desired. I like leaving the skin on for color, but it's a personal preference. Cut eight ½-inch-thick slices from the large base of the eggplant, these will be the eggplant parm rounds. Peel the remaining eggplant if you didn't peel the whole thing and cut into 5 or 6 slices of the same thickness. These slices will be used for making the cheese sauce.

Lay all the slices on wire racks or place in a colander and sprinkle on both sides with 1 teaspoon of the salt. Let the eggplant sit for 20 minutes to release moisture. Gently squeeze excess moisture out by pressing each slice with a clean towel or paper towels.

Sauté the 5 or 6 smaller slices for the cheese sauce in a skillet in the 1 teaspoon olive oil over medium heat for 4 to 5 minutes until very soft, lightly browned, and completely cooked through. Remove from the pan and add to a high-powered blender with the 1 tablespoon olive oil, the remaining ½ teaspoon salt, and the remaining ingredients. Blend until very smooth. Adjust the salt to taste, if necessary.

Meanwhile, to start preparing the saucy spaghetti, bring a large pot of salted water to a boil and cook the spaghetti until al dente. Drain, but do not rinse.

CONTINUED

garnishes

Fresh finely chopped basil,
for garnish (optional)

The Parm

Ground pepper

To fry the remaining eggplant slices, add the vegetable oil to a large cast-iron skillet to a depth of ½ inch. Heat to a temperature of 365°F to 375°F on a deep-frying thermometer.

In a shallow dish, combine the bread crumbs, The Parm, garlic powder, oregano, basil, salt, and pepper. Put the flour and nondairy milk in separate bowls.

Coat an eggplant slice in the flour, next in the nondairy milk, and then in the bread crumb mixture, using your hands to coat it well on all sides and edges.

Fry the breaded eggplant in 2 batches (depending on the size of your pan, but don't overcrowd the slices) for 3 to 4 minutes, flipping halfway through. Set aside on paper towels to soak up any excess oil.

Pour the cheese sauce into a saucepan and heat over medium heat for 4 to 5 minutes, whisking or stirring frequently, allowing the sauce to thicken and become gooey like cheese. Turn off the heat and set aside.

Preheat the oven to broil. Place all the fried eggplant on a baking sheet and spoon about 2 tablespoons of the cheese sauce on each slice, spreading it out to the edges. Broil for 3 to 5 minutes until the cheese bubbles or browns on top. The timing may vary; watch closely so the cheese or eggplant breading don't burn.

Meanwhile, heat the sauce for the spaghetti in a saucepan over a low simmer.

Toss the spaghetti in the sauce while it's still simmering over low heat.

Portion the spaghetti onto plates. Top each serving with 2 cheese-covered eggplant slices. Garnish with fresh basil, more parm, and ground pepper to taste.

hot tip If you want to bake the breaded eggplant slices rather than fry them, line a baking sheet with parchment paper. Place the slices on the sheet and spray with a light coating of oil (this will help with browning). Bake in a preheated 425°F oven for 30 to 40 minutes. Spread the cheese sauce on the slices and broil for 3 to 5 minutes until the cheese bubbles or browns.

butternut squash cannelloni

MAKES 4 servings; 16 to 20 cannelloni
PREP TIME 45 minutes
COOK TIME 90 minutes

prep ahead

The Parm (page 207)

The Mozza (page 208)

roasted butternut squash

2 (2-pound) butternut squashes, peeled and diced (about 8 cups)

2 tablespoons olive oil

½ teaspoon sea salt

½ teaspoon ground pepper

béchamel sauce

½ cup soft tofu

½ cup unsweetened nondairy milk

1 cup low-sodium vegetable stock

2 tablespoons nutritional yeast

2 tablespoons tahini

1 teaspoon miso paste

2 teaspoons cornstarch

½ teaspoon sea salt

1 shallot, minced

2 garlic cloves, minced

1 tablespoon finely chopped fresh sage

¼ teaspoon ground nutmeg

1 tablespoon olive oil

filling

1 cup soft tofu

¾ cup The Parm

Butternut squash is sexy. Wiki tells me she has alter egos in other parts of the world. In Australia and New Zealand she responds to the name butternut pumpkin. What a mysterious vixen! Wherever she goes, she's always the center of attention whether pureed into a soup (page 86) or breaded and fried in our popular tacos (see hotforfoodblog.com). In this recipe she'll sweep you off your feet enveloped in cannelloni and a creamy béchamel that any nonna would approve of!

Preheat the oven to 425°F.

To roast the squash, toss the diced squash in the olive oil, salt, and pepper and arrange on a baking sheet. Bake for 25 minutes until the squash is golden brown, flipping halfway through the bake time.

Meanwhile, to prepare the béchamel sauce, combine the tofu, nondairy milk, ½ cup of the stock, nutritional yeast, tahini, miso paste, cornstarch, and salt in a blender until very smooth.

Heat a saucepan over medium heat and sauté the shallot, garlic, sage, and nutmeg in the olive oil for about 2 minutes until just softened and fragrant. Lower heat if necessary to prevent the garlic from burning. Add the blended tofu mixture and bring to a low simmer, turning the heat back up if needed. As soon as the sauce starts to bubble, stir in the remaining ½ cup stock and bring to a simmer for 1 to 2 minutes until slightly thicker. Pour the sauce into a wide, shallow baking dish.

Once the butternut squash is roasted, turn the oven down to 350°F. Reserve 1 cup of the squash and set aside.

To make the filling, place the remaining squash in a food processor with the filling ingredients and process until smooth.

To fill the cannelloni, transfer the filling to a ziplock bag and snip off a small piece of one corner. Very slowly squeeze the filling into each cannelloni, generously filling it. Arrange the filled cannelloni in 2 rows of 8 or 10 on top of the sauce in the baking dish, spaced ¼ inch apart.

Coarsely chop the reserved butternut squash and arrange on top.

CONTINUED

½ teaspoon ground nutmeg

¼ teaspoon sea salt

¼ teaspoon ground pepper

cannelloli

16 to 20 oven-ready cannelloni

1¼ cups The Mozza

8 whole sage leaves

1 to 2 tablespoons The Parm

Ground pepper

Distribute The Mozza over each row of cannelloni, allowing the ends of the cannelloni to be visible. Top with the sage leaves.

Cover the baking dish with aluminum foil and bake for 45 minutes.

Remove the foil and top the cannelloni with The Parm and pepper to taste. Bake for 15 to 20 minutes on the top rack of the oven until the sauce is golden brown. Watch closely so the topping doesn't burn. You may also need to broil the cannelloni for a few minutes to get The Mozza to brown on top. Serve immediately.

hot tip You can likely find precut fresh or frozen butternut squash if you don't feel like getting intimate with whole squash. But if you use frozen pieces be sure to thaw them and drain any excess water.

bacon mac & cheese skillet

MAKES 4 to 6 servings
PREP TIME 45 minutes
COOK TIME 45 minutes

prep ahead

Mushroom Bacon (page 10), preferably made with shiitakes

The Parm (page 207)

pasta

3 cups elbow macaroni

topping

¼ cup bread crumbs

1 tablespoon The Parm

1 teaspoon dried oregano

1 teaspoon dried basil

1 teaspoon sea salt

Mushroom Bacon

mac & cheese sauce

1 cup raw cashews, soaked in hot water for 20 minutes

2¼ cups unsweetened nondairy milk

⅓ cup vegetable oil

⅓ cup nutritional yeast

¼ cup freshly squeezed lemon juice

3 tablespoons tomato paste

1½ tablespoons miso paste

2 teaspoons chili powder

2 teaspoons onion powder

2 teaspoons garlic powder

2 teaspoons arrowroot or tapioca flour

1 teaspoon sea salt

½ teaspoon ground white pepper or black pepper

It's the best mac & cheese ever! Says anyone who's tried our classic version. Just a couple of tweaks and some smoky shiitake bacon thrown into the mix and we have ourselves a real winner! Anyone who knows me (in real life or online) knows that my obsession for mac & cheese is fierce, unrelenting, and maybe even a bit of a problem. I dream about swimming in it! Hands down, I'm like a sommelier for vegan mac & cheese. So trust me on this one—don't mess with it. You'll be tempted to, 'cause I know you. But don't. Once you pour that cheese sauce in the skillet, it will be near overflowing. You literally COULD swim in the skillet there's that much cheese sauce. Don't omit any amount of it, unless you like disappointment.

Preheat the oven to 350°F.

To cook the pasta, bring a pot of salted water to a boil. Cook the pasta until al dente. Drain, but do not rinse.

To prepare the topping, combine the bread crumbs, The Parm, herbs, and salt in a small bowl.

To make the sauce, drain and rinse the cashews. Add to a high-powered blender with the remaining ingredients and blend on high until very smooth.

In a 9-inch cast-iron skillet or baking dish, stir the pasta and sauce together until the macaroni is well coated. What looks like an excess amount of sauce will thicken during baking!

Sprinkle three-fourths of the bread crumb mixture evenly on top. Sprinkle the bacon pieces liberally on top. Press them slightly into the bread crumb layer but keep them still visible. Top with the remaining bread crumbs.

Cover with aluminum foil and bake for 20 minutes.

Remove the foil and bake on the top rack of the oven for 10 minutes until the top is golden brown and the sides are bubbling slightly. Depending on your oven and the distribution of heat, you might want to set the skillet under the broiler for 5 minutes to get the top crispier instead of continuing to bake at 350°F. Serve immediately. When reheating leftovers you may want to add more nondairy milk to get it creamy once again.

the best vegan ramen

MAKES 4 generous servings
PREP TIME 45 minutes
COOK TIME 2 hours

prep ahead

Tofu Bacon Crumbles
(page 10), optional

broth

2 onions, halved

2 garlic bulbs

2 large sweet potatoes, diced

2 tablespoons vegetable oil

1 pound cremini mushrooms

8 ounces shiitake mushrooms

2 celery stalks, quartered

3 green onions, quartered

2 thick slices of fresh ginger

½ head of napa cabbage, quartered

1 tablespoon sea salt

1 tablespoon ground pepper

1 large piece kombu seaweed

12 cups water

tare

⅓ cup low-sodium tamari or soy sauce

⅓ cup tahini

2 tablespoons red or white miso paste

1 tablespoon seasoned rice vinegar or mirin

noodles & toppings

4 (3 oz/100 g) packs vegan-friendly ramen noodles

1 carrot, shredded or ribboned

1 cup frozen corn, thawed and drained

I'm half Japanese, but I'm not going to front like I'm some kind of ramen expert. I even read we stole it from China! Anyway this isn't a history lesson. You just want noodles drowning in a well-rounded, rich, layered umami broth. So I've created a homemade ramen that's less intimidating to make but just as decadent and flavorful as anything you'd order in a restaurant. And the best part, of course, is it's all veggie based! The tare is your main squeeze here. It's where all the flavor exists, bringing the salty, sweet, sour, and spiciness to this dish or, rather, umami!

Some things to keep in mind: You'll need a large stockpot that can hold 6 quarts or more to make the broth. I've listed The Tofu Bacon Crumbles as optional, but they're like a fried pork substitute and are really tasty in this dish. The broth and tare can be made ahead and refrigerated—you will reheat the broth but do not heat the tare. The tare is meant to have hot liquid poured over it rather than being heated in the stockpot. If you heat it in the stockpot, it will separate and cloud rather than meshing nicely into the broth. This recipe is slightly more time-consuming than the others but certainly not difficult to make.

To make the broth, preheat the oven to 450°F.

On a large baking sheet, arrange the onion halves, garlic bulbs, and diced sweet potatoes. Roast for 40 minutes until the potatoes are cooked through and there is charring on the vegetables.

Heat the vegetable oil in a large stockpot over medium heat and combine the mushrooms, celery, green onions, ginger, and cabbage. Add the roasted onion halves and 1 of the roasted garlic bulbs (smashing it a bit to release the roasted garlic). Sauté for 10 minutes until the vegetables are wilted and cooked down a little. Add the salt, pepper, kombu, and water. Bring to a boil, then lower the heat, cover, and simmer for 1 hour.

Meanwhile combine the tare ingredients together until smooth and set aside. This can last in the fridge for up to 1 month but do not freeze it. It's best to make the tare as you need it.

4 green onions, sliced diagonally

1 cup warmed Tofu Bacon (optional)

3 teaspoons chile oil or sesame oil (optional)

Strain the broth into a large bowl or another pot that can hold about 11 cups liquid. If you see any roasted garlic still intact, reserve the soft cloves, removing the skins. You can also reserve the mushrooms and add to the final bowls of ramen. Compost the strained the vegetables! Clean the stockpot and add the strained broth back in.

In a blender, combine ½ cup of the roasted sweet potatoes with 1 cup of the strained broth, the roasted cloves from the remaining garlic bulb, and any roasted cloves you pulled from the broth. Blend until smooth and cloudy. Then add this mixture to the stockpot of broth.

To cook the noodles, bring the finished broth to a boil in the stockpot. Add the noodles and lower heat to a simmer. They will take about 3 minutes to cook. If you're not serving all the portions at the same time, only use the amount of broth and noodles you need. Alternatively you can cook the ramen in a separate pot of boiling water. Drain but do not rinse. Then add them into the heated broth at serving. Store the remaining broth in the fridge and consume within 7 days or freeze for up to 2 months.

Traditionally bowls are warmed before serving. You can heat them in a microwave or, if they're oven-safe, in a 325°F oven for a few minutes, but it's not necessary. You can also reheat the remaining roasted sweet potato.

To serve, place 2 tablespoons of the tare in the bottom of each bowl. Top with 1 cup of the broth. Stir with a chopstick to mix together. Fill with approximately 1½ cups of the broth, depending on the size of the bowl, and add a portion of noodles. Top each serving with shredded carrot, corn, green onion, remaining sweet potato, and bacon crumbles. Drizzle with chile oil, if desired, or with sesame oil if you don't want spice.

the main event

Certainly anything in this book can be eaten as a main course because, again, there are no rules! But most cookbooks include a chapter highlighting "meaty" main dishes. Well, here's my contribution in that department, and I think this is the perfect chapter to show off to people who are dumbfounded as to what a vegan eats. Just look at the variety of meals inspired by cuisines from all around the world. And I couldn't resist adding a deep-fried avocado, just 'cause! This is a great place to start if you're looking to adopt Meatless Mondays or need to switch up the usual dinner routine.

stuffed crust pizza

MAKES 8 to 10 slices
PREP TIME 30 minutes, plus up to 1 hour for proofing
COOK TIME 35 minutes

prep ahead

That Dough (page 168)

Vegan Bangers (page 161)

ingredients

That Dough

2 to 3 tablespoons olive oil

4 cups vegan mozzarella shreds

3 Vegan Bangers, premade vegan sausage, or vegan pepperoni, sliced

½ cup pizza sauce

½ red onion, sliced

1 cup broccoli florets, finely chopped (about ½ crown)

½ teaspoon red pepper flakes

Pizza with cheese-stuffed crust changed the world in the '90s, so why should now be any different? I honestly don't care what you put on this pizza or what you stuff inside the crust—just know that pizza crust always deserves your attention and that this one is begging to be stuffed. When I see people dispose of their pizza crust, I want to scream! That's the best part. So I figure stuffing it might entice you to see your slice through to the end, because it means you get a bonus surprise: more succulent bread and cheese. Oh, and if you're real sassy, you could always throw some Tofu Bacon Crumbles (page 10) in there too!

Preheat the oven to 475°F.

For this recipe, you let the dough rise to double in size. Roll out the dough on a floured work surface to an 18-inch circle. Transfer to a 16-inch aerated pizza pan coated with some of the olive oil. The crust should hang off the edge of the pan. You can also place the dough on a pizza paddle if you're transferring it to a pizza stone in your oven.

Place 2 cups of the mozzarella shreds around the edge of the dough and fold the dough over the cheese, lightly pressing it into the bottom of the pan to seal.

If you're using the bangers, brown the slices in a skillet over medium heat with a bit of the olive oil for 4 to 5 minutes.

Top the pizza with the sauce, brushing some onto the folded edge. Then top with 1 cup of the cheese shreds and half of the onion, broccoli, and bangers. Top with the remaining 1 cup mozzarella shreds and the remaining onion, broccoli, and bangers. Sprinkle with the red pepper flakes. Brush the crust with a light coating of the remaining olive oil.

Bake for 20 minutes until the crust and bottom of the pizza are golden brown. Let rest for 10 minutes, then slice with a pizza cutter and serve.

loaded fries supreme

MAKES 2 entrée servings
or 4 side servings
PREP TIME 30 minutes
COOK TIME 1 hour

prep ahead

Tofu Bacon Crumbles (page 10)

The Nacho Cheese (page 205)

The Sour Cream (page 210)

french fries

4 russet potatoes

¼ cup vegetable oil

1 teaspoon paprika

1 teaspoon sea salt

½ teaspoon ground pepper

toppings

The Nacho Cheese

½ cup The Sour Cream

Tofu Bacon Crumbles

2 vine tomatoes, seeds removed and diced

1 tablespoon finely chopped chives

This isn't a mirage of fast food you can't eat! While it looks like a guilt-laden dish of french fries smothered with cheese, sour cream, and bacon, it is—except it's made with simple plant-based ingredients so there's absolutely nothing to feel bad about. Have your fries plain or loaded to the max like this whenever the craving hits.

Preheat the oven to 425°F.

To make the french fries, wash the potatoes and cut into approximately ½-inch matchsticks, leaving the skin on. Place in a large pot of cold water and bring to a boil. Cook until you can just pierce the surface with a fork, 6 to 8 minutes. The potatoes shouldn't be too tender or soft.

Line 2 baking sheets with parchment paper. Drain the water from the pot and toss the potatoes with the vegetable oil, paprika, salt, and pepper until evenly coated. Lay them out on the baking sheets spaced ¼ inch apart; do not overcrowd.

Bake for 45 to 50 minutes, flipping the fries halfway through the bake time, until golden brown and crisp.

Split the fries among serving plates, layering them with nacho cheese and sour cream. Top with the bacon crumbles, tomatoes, and chives.

orange tofu & veggie fried rice

MAKES 4 to 6 servings
PREP TIME 50 minutes
COOK TIME 45 minutes

fried rice

1½ cups long-grain white rice

2½ cups water

¾ teaspoon sea salt

2 tablespoons vegetable oil

2 green onions, white and green parts, thinly sliced diagonally

2 garlic cloves, minced

½ cup finely chopped carrot (about ½ carrot)

2 cups finely chopped broccoli florets (about 1 crown)

½ cup frozen peas

½ cup frozen corn

1 vegan chicken-flavored bouillon cube dissolved in 3 tablespoons hot water, or 3 tablespoons low-sodium vegetable stock

1 tablespoon low-sodium tamari or soy sauce

¼ teaspoon ground pepper

orange sauce

1 tablespoon vegetable oil

2 garlic cloves, minced

2 teaspoons minced fresh ginger

2 green onions, white parts only, finely chopped

¼ teaspoon red pepper flakes

1 teaspoon grated orange zest

¼ cup freshly squeezed orange juice

¼ cup low-sodium tamari or soy sauce

¼ cup unseasoned rice vinegar

½ cup sugar

1 cup plus 1 tablespoon water

1 tablespoon cornstarch

When those Chinese food cravings come rolling in, turn to this page and stare at the photo before logging on to order takeout. Within seconds you'll realize that putting in the bit of effort it takes to make this simple crispy orange tofu and quick fried rice is completely worth it. It's mega tasty and fresh and a great way to fry up extra veggies you have lying around too.

To cook the rice, combine the rice, water, and ½ teaspoon of the salt, cover, and bring to a boil. Stir, cover again, lower the heat to a simmer, and cook for 10 to 15 minutes. Adjust the water and cooking times to your particular brand of rice! You need 4 to 5 cups cooked rice.

To make the orange sauce, in a saucepan, heat the vegetable oil over medium-low heat and sauté the garlic, ginger, green onions, and red pepper flakes for 1 to 2 minutes. Add the orange zest and juice, tamari, vinegar, sugar, and 1 cup water. Bring to a simmer and cook for 10 minutes. In a small bowl, combine the cornstarch and 1 tablespoon water into a slurry and whisk into the sauce until thickened. Remove from the heat and set aside.

To make the fried tofu, drain the tofu and cut into bite-size cubes. Allow the cubes to sit on a tea towel or paper towels to get rid of the excess water.

Heat the vegetable oil in a heavy-bottomed pot or deep fryer to a temperature of 365°F to 375°F on a deep-frying thermometer. You'll need about 2 inches of oil; the amount of oil may vary if using a deep fryer.

In a bowl, combine the rice flour, cornstarch, salt, garlic powder, and pepper. Do not add the club soda until the oil is ready. When you're ready to fry, fold the soda into the flour mixture but do not overmix.

Using your hands, coat batches of the tofu cubes in the batter and delicately drop each one into the hot oil. Fry for 2 to 2½ minutes. If some stick together, gently separate them with a slotted frying spoon. Remove the crispy tofu from the oil with the slotted spoon to paper towels to absorb excess oil. Continue this process to fry the remaining tofu cubes.

CONTINUED

fried tofu

2 bricks (16 oz/450 g each) medium-firm tofu

4 to 6 cups vegetable oil, for frying

1 cup brown rice flour

1 tablespoon cornstarch

½ teaspoon sea salt

½ teaspoon garlic powder

¼ teaspoon ground pepper

1 cup cold club soda

To finish the fried rice, heat a large skillet or wok over medium-high heat with the vegetable oil and sauté the green onions (reserving some for a garnish), garlic, carrot, broccoli, peas, and corn for 5 minutes until softened and slightly browned. Adjust the heat to avoid burning the garlic. Add the cooked rice, stock, tamari, pepper, and remaining ¼ teaspoon salt. Continue cooking for 5 to 6 minutes, stirring occasionally, until the rice has some crispy parts and the vegetables are cooked but still bright in color. You can cook the rice longer if you prefer.

Just before the rice is finished, heat the orange sauce to a simmer if it has cooled down. Remove it from the heat and pour into a bowl. Toss batches of the crispy tofu in the sauce, coating them evenly.

Garnish the tofu with the reserved green onions and serve over the fried rice.

fried avocados with jackfruit

MAKES 6 servings, 12 pieces
PREP TIME 40 minutes
COOK TIME 45 minutes

prep ahead

The Classic Ranch (page 223)

beer-braised jackfruit

2 cans young jackfruit in water or brine (not syrup)

1 cup thinly sliced onion (about 1 onion)

1 tablespoon vegetable oil

½ cup finely chopped red bell pepper (about ½ pepper)

1 cup finely chopped pineapple

2 teaspoons minced fresh ginger

2 garlic cloves, minced

½ teaspoon red pepper flakes

Grated zest and juice of 1 lime

2 tablespoons vegan Worcestershire

1 cup vegan-friendly lager or ale or 1 cup vegetable stock

fried avocados

4 to 6 cups vegetable oil, for deep-frying

¾ cup all-purpose flour

1 cup unsweetened nondairy milk

1½ cups bread crumbs

1 teaspoon garlic powder

1 teaspoon chipotle chile powder or chile powder

1 teaspoon sea salt

½ teaspoon ground cumin

6 ripe but firm avocados

This dish started out as a whole avocado stuffed and then deep-fried, which worked, but it really wasn't much to look at and was difficult to eat. But frying the halves of an avo and stuffing them with this delectable meaty jackfruit worked out much better. I have no idea what this is, except a fun dinner party or potluck idea to show off and gloat about how much of a kitchen wizard you are. The real skill is in timing the execution of this recipe so the ripeness of the avocados is perfect . . . not too hard and not too soft. If the avocados are too ripe and mushy, it won't work!

To make the beer-braised jackfruit, drain the jackfruit and rinse well. Squeeze out the excess liquid from the fruit through a sieve if the fruit seems excessively watery. Pat dry with paper towels.

Heat a cast-iron skillet or pan over medium heat and sauté the onion in the vegetable oil for 3 minutes until just softened. Add the bell pepper, pineapple, ginger, garlic, and red pepper flakes and sauté for 6 minutes.

Add the jackfruit and sauté for another 3 to 4 minutes until lightly browned.

Add the lime zest and juice, Worcestershire, and lager. Stir to combine and bring to a simmer. Once the mixture is bubbling, adjust the heat to medium-low, cover, and cook for 20 minutes, stirring occasionally. Once most of the liquid is absorbed, turn off the heat but leave covered to stay warm.

To fry the avocados, heat the vegetable oil in a heavy-bottomed pot or deep fryer to a temperature of 365°F to 375°F on a deep-frying thermometer.

Place the all-purpose flour in a bowl and the nondairy milk in another bowl. In a third bowl, combine the bread crumbs, garlic powder, chipotle chile powder, salt, and cumin.

Cut each avocado in half. Remove the pit. Gently peel the skin from the halves. Carefully scoop a small amount of avocado from the center of each half to create more of a bowl, leaving the sides intact.

CONTINUED

Serve with

The Classic Ranch

1 handful fresh cilantro, chopped (optional)

1 lime, cut into wedges (optional)

Coat each avocado half in the all-purpose flour, shaking off any excess, then immerse in the nondairy milk. Toss in the bread crumb mixture. Use your hands to gently press and pack on the crumb mixture so the entire half is well coated.

To avoid overcrowding the pot, fry 2 halves at a time for 2 minutes until golden brown. Remove with a slotted frying spoon or tongs, allowing any excess oil to drip off before placing the halves on a plate or baking sheet lined with paper towels.

To serve, scoop a generous portion of the jackfruit on top of each avocado half. Top with the ranch dressing. Add cilantro and a drizzle of extra lime juice, if desired.

hot tip You might have seen packaged marinated jackfruit with different seasonings and sauces in grocery stores. It just has to be heated, so feel free to use that instead of making your own!

hot tip Nut-free folks can blend the verde sauce with the thick cream from the top of a can (13.5 oz/400 ml) of full-fat coconut milk instead of using cashews!

bean & cheese enchiladas verdes

MAKES 4 servings
PREP TIME 50 minutes
COOK TIME 25 minutes

verde sauce

- ½ cup raw cashews, soaked in hot water for 20 minutes
- 1½ cups salsa verde
- 1 tablespoon freshly squeezed lime juice
- ½ cup packed fresh cilantro leaves (optional)

enchiladas

- 3 tablespoons plus 1 teaspoon vegetable oil
- ½ cup finely chopped onion (about ½ onion)
- 2 garlic cloves, minced
- ½ teaspoon chipotle chile powder
- ½ teaspoon chile powder
- ½ teaspoon sea salt
- ¼ teaspoon ground pepper
- 1 cup frozen corn, thawed and drained
- 4 cups spinach
- 1 cup cooked navy beans or 1 can (15 oz/425 g) navy beans, rinsed and drained
- 1½ cups vegan mozzarella shreds
- 12 (6-inch) corn tortillas
- 1 jalapeño chile, thinly sliced and seeded

toppings

- 1 avocado, pitted, peeled, and diced
- 1 green onion, white and green parts, finely chopped
- Handful fresh cilantro, coarsely chopped, for garnish
- Salsa verde, for serving
- Lime wedges, for serving

If you're saucy like me, you'll adore these bean and cheese enchiladas! They're stuffed to the max and drenched in a spicy, creamy, fresh green sauce. Since dairy is no longer my deal, I'm always ready to party with cashews, and I'm obsessed with this sauce! Combining the silkiness of cashews with salsa verde puts these lil' rolls over the top!

To make the verde sauce, drain and rinse the cashews. Add to a high-powered blender along with the salsa verde, lime juice, and cilantro. Blend on high until very smooth. Set aside.

Preheat the oven to 375°F. Lightly oil a rectangular baking dish about 12 by 8 inches with 1 teaspoon of the vegetable oil.

To prepare the enchiladas, heat a skillet over medium heat with 1 tablespoon of the vegetable oil and sauté the onion and garlic for 2 minutes until just softened. Stir in the chipotle chile powder, salt, and pepper and cook for another minute. Add the corn and spinach and cook for about 2 minutes until the corn is cooked and the spinach is soft and wilted but still bright green. Stir in the beans and 1 cup mozzarella shreds and cook for another 2 minutes. Remove the filling from the pan to a dish and set aside.

Wipe out the pan and set over medium-low heat. Coat the pan with another tablespoon vegetable oil and heat the tortillas in small batches for 1 to 2 minutes, flipping as needed. Add the remaining tablespoon of vegetable oil if necessary for the next batches to get the tortillas softened and lightly coated in oil.

Pour a small amount of the verde sauce into the bottom of the oiled baking dish, spreading it out to coat the bottom.

Place about a scant ¼ cup filling on each tortilla, roll tightly, and arrange seam side down in the dish. Make 2 rows of filled tortillas.

Pour the remaining verde sauce over the enchiladas and top with the remaining ½ cup of the mozzarella shreds and the jalapeño slices. Bake for 15 minutes until the cheese has melted and the edges of the tortillas are just turning golden brown.

Top with the diced avocado, green onion, and cilantro. Serve immediately with salsa verde and lime wedges!

bbq tofu and jalapeño-lime aioli slaw
from banh mi bowl (page 64)

guacamole (page 156)

when in doubt . . . .
put it in a taco!

You know my motto! Rather than create yet another taco recipe, of which the blog has many, I figured you could take some inspo from this taco vision board. Tasty morsels and components from this book can easily be reimagined into customized tacos whenever you damn please! Pair fillings from the Finger Foods (page 33), Veggie Sides & Big Salads (page 55), Stacked Sandwiches (page 90), and The Main Event (page 137) chapters with your fave sauces and go to town. See you next Taco Tuesday!

fajita sauté, guacamole, and sour cream
from fajita fiesta bowls (page 156)

oyster mushrooms and thousand island from oyster mushroom po' boy (page 92)

the sour cream (page 210)

the nacho cheese (page 205)

bbq jackfruit, slaw, and pickled red onions from bbq jackfruit sandwich (page 107)

sweet potato gnocchi

MAKES 6 to 8 servings
PREP TIME 70 minutes
COOK TIME 50 minutes

prep ahead

The Parm (page 207)

ingredients

2 pounds peeled, cubed sweet potatoes (2 to 3 potatoes)

2 teaspoons sea salt

⅛ teaspoon ground nutmeg

⅛ teaspoon ground cinnamon

1½ to 2 cups all-purpose flour

6 to 8 tablespoons olive oil

6 garlic cloves, minced

3 tablespoons finely chopped fresh sage

4 cups stemmed, finely chopped Lacinato kale

¼ cup freshly squeezed lemon juice

Ground pepper

The Parm

Just Google "gnocchi," and you'll find many many methods and rules for how it should be made and handled. When I decided to test it for this cookbook, it was so much easier than chefy types have led me to believe. The pros are onto something, though, with using a ricer or food mill, but you can get away with mashing your potatoes by hand. I'd say you better be in touch with your spirit guides for this one kids, 'cause you're going to be relying on some cosmic intuition to know when the dough has been handled just enough, has the perfect amount of flour, and is ready to be made into soft pillowy morsels for your mouth. So it's a good thing I took pictures for you! It's honestly not as hard as you might think.

To make the dough, bring a pot of cold water with the cubed sweet potatoes and 1 teaspoon of the salt to a boil. Cook until a fork easily pierces the sweet potatoes, 8 to 10 minutes. Drain the potatoes well and let cool.

Pass the potatoes through a food mill or ricer onto a work surface. Or mash with a potato masher, being sure there are no big chunks of potato. You will need about 2½ cups mashed potatoes.

Sprinkle the potatoes with the nutmeg, cinnamon, remaining 1 teaspoon salt, and 1 cup of the flour. Using your hands and the help of a dough cutter or spatula, fold the mixture in overlapping layers a few times until most of the flour is mixed in.

Add ½ to 1 cup of the remaining flour to the dough while folding but do not overmix or add too much flour. You should still see flour as you fold the dough the last couple of times. The dough should still feel fairly soft and resemble potato but be able to hold its shape. Shape the dough into a loaf and let it rest on a floured surface for 10 to 15 minutes.

Flour another area of your work surface for cutting and shaping the gnocchi. Flour 2 baking sheets to hold the gnocchi.

CONTINUED

Make sure your hands are generously floured. Flatten the dough into a ½-inch-thick rectangle approximately 6 inches by 9 inches. Flour a sharp knife or a dough cutter and cut the rectangle lengthwise into nine 1-inch-thick rows. Cut each row in half into strips. Roll out each strip into a rope about ¾ inch in diameter. Cut crosswise into small pieces just slightly wider than ½ inch. You will have 140 to 160 pieces.

Place the pieces on the floured baking sheets and cover with tea towels. You should boil the gnocchi soon after making them, or you can freeze the uncooked gnocchi between layers of parchment paper in airtight containers for up to 3 months. Cook the frozen gnocchi, without thawing, as directed below when ready to serve.

To cook the gnocchi, bring a pot of salted water to a boil. Place batches of the gnocchi in the boiling water. They will take 2 to 3 minutes to cook and will float to the top. Remove with a slotted spoon onto a large platter or place the batches directly in a hot skillet to continue cooking.

While the gnocchi are boiling, heat a cast-iron skillet or nonstick pan over medium-low heat with 1 tablespoon of olive oil. Sauté 1 or 2 cloves of the minced garlic, 2 teaspoons of the sage, and a small handful of the kale for 1 to 2 minutes until the garlic is soft and fragrant and the kale has just started to wilt. Add a batch of the gnocchi and about 2 teaspoons of the lemon juice. Brown the gnocchi 3 to 4 minutes on each side. Remove to serving dishes, season with salt and pepper, and top with The Parm to taste.

Cook the gnocchi in batches of 1 or 2 servings depending on the size of your pan, but don't overcrowd it. Add more olive oil to the pan to cook the next batches in the same fashion.

fajita fiesta bowls

MAKES 4 servings
PREP TIME 35 minutes
COOK TIME 25 minutes

prep ahead

The Sour Cream (page 210)

salsa

1 cup finely diced tomato

¼ cup finely chopped red onion

¼ cup chopped fresh cilantro

Juice of ½ lime

Sea salt and ground pepper

lime rice

1½ cups long-grain white rice

2 cups water

1 garlic clove, minced

½ teaspoon sea salt

Juice of ½ lime

¼ cup chopped fresh cilantro

fajita sauté

1 cup thinly sliced red bell pepper

1 cup thinly sliced green bell pepper

1 cup thinly sliced red onion

4 large portobello mushrooms, sliced (about 3 cups)

2 tablespoons vegetable oil

1 teaspoon chipotle chile powder

1 teaspoon sea salt

½ teaspoon ground pepper

guacamole

1 large or 2 small ripe avocados

Juice of 1 lime

Sea salt and ground pepper

serve with

2 cups frozen corn, thawed and drained

The Sour Cream

Veggie fajitas are usually one of two options a vegan has to choose from at a nonvegan restaurant chain. But I've always loved them! I think I have an affinity for that hot sizzling skillet that arrives at the table steaming up in my face. Since deconstructing is my thang, here's a fajita in bowl form that makes an easy lunch or dinner when you're having a busy week. Feel free to serve with tortillas just like typical fajitas if you're feelin' it, and you can definitely throw a side of refried beans in the mix too! Garnish with additional cilantro, if desired.

To make the salsa, combine the tomato, onion, cilantro, and lime juice in a bowl. Season to taste with salt and pepper. Refrigerate until ready to serve.

To make the lime rice, combine the rice, water, garlic, and salt in a pot, cover, and bring to a boil. Stir, cover again, lower the heat to a simmer, and cook for 10 to 15 minutes. While the rice is still warm, stir in the lime juice and cilantro. Set aside and keep covered. Adjust the water and cooking time for your particular brand of rice!

To make the fajita sauté, in a skillet over medium-high heat, sauté the bell peppers, onion, and portobellos with the vegetable oil for 3 minutes until the peppers and onions are just softened and the mushrooms are releasing moisture. Add the chipotle chile powder, salt, and pepper and continue cooking for 3 to 4 minutes until most of the liquid has evaporated or until cooked to your liking.

Make the guacamole right before assembling bowls. Halve and pit the avocados. Scoop the avocado flesh into a bowl and mash with the lime juice, salt, and pepper to taste.

For each serving, place a bed of lime rice in a bowl. Top with the sautéed vegetables, corn, salsa, and guacamole. Garnish with the sour cream.

waffle-topped cottage pie

MAKES 4 servings
PREP TIME 45 minutes
COOK TIME 70 minutes

prep ahead

The Gravy (page 220), optional

mashed potatoes

2 pounds potatoes, peeled and cubed

1 teaspoon sea salt

½ teaspoon ground pepper

⅛ teaspoon paprika

2 tablespoons finely chopped chives

filling

1 cup finely chopped onion (about 1 onion)

½ cup finely chopped carrot (about ½ carrot)

2 tablespoons vegetable oil

2 garlic cloves, minced

1 teaspoon fresh thyme leaves

½ teaspoon ground sage

½ teaspoon sea salt

½ teaspoon ground pepper

5 cups coarsely chopped cremini mushrooms (about 10 ounces)

2 tablespoons vegan Worcestershire

2 teaspoons tomato paste

1 cup fresh or frozen corn

1 cup fresh or frozen peas

2 cups cooked lentils, or 1 (19 oz/539 g) can lentils, rinsed and drained

1 tablespoon cornstarch

1 tablespoon water

I told you how life changing buying a waffle iron was, but if you have yet to throw mashed potatoes in there you're in for a sweet surprise. In fact you might never eat mashed potatoes the same way again! They taste a thousand times better when they crisp up and have little pockets to store pools of sauce or gravy. Not to mention, they're such an impeccable topping to modernize an old-fashioned cottage pie.

To make the mashed potatoes, bring a large pot of cold water with the potatoes to a boil. Cook until tender, 10 to 12 minutes. Drain the potatoes and mash in the pot with the salt, pepper, and paprika. Fold in the chives. If you're not making waffles, you can use the mashed potatoes on individual servings or on top of a larger baking dish, but I would add some nondairy milk and/or vegan butter or vegetable oil to make the mash smoother. However, it needs to be dry like this for crispy potato waffles.

Preheat the oven to 400°F. For individual servings use four 8-ounce ramekins or an 8-inch square baking dish for a single pie.

To make the filling, sauté the onion and carrot in a skillet with the vegetable oil over medium heat for 3 minutes until just softened. Add the garlic, thyme, sage, salt, and pepper and continue to cook for 2 minutes.

Add the mushrooms and cook, stirring occasionally, for 5 minutes until just over halfway cooked.

Add the Worcestershire, tomato paste, corn, peas, and lentils and stir to coat well. Cook for about 3 minutes until the corn and peas are cooked through, but the peas are still bright green.

Mix the cornstarch with the water to make a slurry and add it along with the stock to the pan, stirring until well combined. Simmer for 3 to 4 minutes until the filling is thickened and only a small amount of excess liquid remains in the pan.

CONTINUED

1 cup low-sodium vegetable stock, or ½ vegan beef-flavored bouillon cube dissolved in 1 cup hot water

Topping
The Gravy, warmed

If using ramekins, place them on a baking sheet and portion the filling among the ramekins. If you're not making waffles, place the filling in the baking dish, the mashed potatoes on top, and bake for 20 minutes until the top is golden brown and the filling is bubbling.

To cook the waffles, heat up your waffle iron and spray it with a light coating of oil. Use a heaping ¾ cup potatoes per waffle and cook for 7 to 8 minutes until golden brown and crispy. This amount will not fill the entire waffle iron but make a size reasonable to fit on top of the 4 to 4½-inch wide ramekins. The time may vary, depending on the make of your waffle iron. Place the crispy potato waffles on a wire rack until all are done. Set a waffle on each ramekin and bake for 10 minutes. Serve immediately with warm gravy on top, if desired!

bangers & mash

MAKES 4 servings; 8 sausages
PREP TIME 40 minutes, plus curing bangers overnight
COOK TIME 1 hour

prep ahead

The Gravy (page 220)

vegan bangers

1 cup sliced onion (about 1 onion)

2 garlic cloves, minced

1 teaspoon fennel seeds

½ teaspoon red pepper flakes

4 tablespoons vegetable oil

2 cups vital wheat gluten

1 cup crumbled firm tofu

¼ cup nutritional yeast

1 teaspoon sea salt

1 teaspoon ground pepper

1 teaspoon smoked paprika

1 teaspoon ground mustard

1 tablespoon maple syrup

2 tablespoons low-sodium tamari or soy sauce

1 tablespoon tomato paste

½ teaspoon liquid smoke

mashed potatoes

3 pounds potatoes, peeled and cubed

¼ cup vegan butter

½ cup unsweetened nondairy milk

1 teaspoon sea salt

1 teaspoon ground pepper

2 tablespoons finely chopped chives

These homemade seitan sausages that I Frankensteined have slightly different seasonings and texture than the Saved By Seitan (page 95) sandwich meat. They are basically identical to my favorite brand of vegan sausages . . . nah, they're better! Of course, I can't tell you what brand that is because #notsponsored. However, making these yourself is highly rewarding. You'll just need to let them sit overnight in the fridge so plan accordingly. We've added them on top of the Stuffed Crust Pizza (page 139), but you can make different sizes for hot dogs or breakfast sausages. Shape them longer and skinnier for hot dogs and grill or panfry them in BBQ sauce. For breakfast sausages, make small patties or smaller sausage links and panfry them in a light coating of maple syrup. It's a real sausage party here!

To make the bangers, preheat the oven to 350°F.

In a skillet over medium heat, sauté the onion, garlic, fennel seeds, and red pepper flakes in 1 tablespoon of the vegetable oil for 4 to 5 minutes until the onions are soft and translucent. Lower the heat as necessary to prevent the garlic from burning.

Add the onion mixture to a food processor along with the 2 tablespoons vegetable oil, 1 cup of the vital wheat gluten, and the remaining ingredients. Process until mostly combined. Add the remaining 1 cup vital wheat gluten and process until the dough forms a ball and is mostly combined. Place the dough on a work surface and knead 10 to 15 times until well combined.

Cut 8 pieces of aluminum foil approximately 10 by 12 inches. Place a portion of the sausage dough in the center of each piece of foil and form into a log shape approximately 1½ inches wide and 4½ inches long. Wrap tightly, twisting the ends in opposite directions to seal the foil firmly around the dough and shape it into a sausage.

Place all the wrapped sausages on a baking sheet spaced an inch apart and bake for 30 minutes until they feel very firm to touch. Let cool for 20 to 30 minutes at room temperature. They might still be warm, but

CONTINUED

BANGERS & MASH *continued*

Serve with

The Gravy

1 ½ cups frozen peas

then refrigerate them at least overnight. Refrigeration is absolutely necessary; otherwise the gluten will not activate and the sausage texture will not be right!

Prepare the mashed potatoes just before serving. Bring a large pot of cold water with the potatoes to a boil. Cook until tender, 10 to 12 minutes. Drain and mash in the pot with the remaining ingredients.

Just before serving, heat up the gravy in a saucepan and thin out with water or vegetable stock if necessary.

To cook the bangers, heat a skillet over medium heat with the remaining 1 tablespoon of vegetable oil and panfry the sausages for 5 to 6 minutes until browned on all sides. Add about ¼ cup of the gravy to coat the sausages and cook for 1 more minute. You can add the peas at the end to cook through or steam them separately.

Plate the dish with a heaping mound of potatoes, 2 sausages, peas, and more gravy on top. Serve immediately!

mushroom, leek & tomato risotto

MAKES 4 to 6 servings
PREP TIME 25 minutes
COOK TIME 35 minutes

prep ahead

The Parm (page 207)

ingredients

3 vegan chicken-flavored bouillon cubes dissolved in 6 cups hot water, or 6 cups low-sodium vegetable stock

1 leek, halved and sliced thin

2 tablespoons vegan butter

8 ounces button mushrooms (about 2 heaping cups)

¼ teaspoon sea salt

¼ teaspoon ground pepper

2 tablespoons finely chopped sundried tomatoes

2 cups Arborio rice

1 cup dry white wine

½ cup The Parm, plus more for garnish

¼ cup packed basil leaves, finely chopped, plus more for garnish

3 teaspoons freshly squeezed lemon juice

1 thinly sliced green onion (green parts only), for garnish

Cooking is a form of meditation for me, and comfort food like risotto forces me (and you!) to be present for the whole process of bringing it to life. You gotta give it love from start to finish, so Instagram breaks are forbidden during this session, k? This risotto is creamy, super savory, and even cheesy. The Parm works its magic in this dish and meshes nicely with the sundried tomatoes, leek, and cute button mushrooms. Now, take a deep breath in, and go!

It's important that the stock for cooking the rice be hot, so heat it in a saucepan and have it ready to be ladled into the risotto as you go.

In a stockpot over medium heat, sauté the leek in the butter for 2 to 3 minutes until just softened. Add the mushrooms and cook for another 2 minutes. Add the salt and pepper and continue cooking for approximately 4 minutes.

Stir in the sundried tomatoes and rice. Stir constantly for 3 to 4 minutes to release the starch in the rice. Add the white wine and simmer, stirring constantly, for 3 to 4 minutes until most of the wine is absorbed.

Add ¼ cup of The Parm and stir until combined into the rice mixture. Add 1 cup of the stock and stir constantly until mostly absorbed.

Add another ¼ cup of The Parm and another 1 cup of the stock. Continue stirring constantly until the liquid is absorbed. Add 3 cups of the stock, 1 cup at a time, stirring constantly after each addition until the liquid is absorbed.

Stir in the ¼ cup basil and the remaining 1 cup stock and stir constantly until the liquid is absorbed. At this point, check your risotto. It shouldn't be too mushy and the rice should have a bit of a bite but still be tender. Turn off the heat and stir in the lemon juice.

Serve immediately with more of The Parm sprinkled on top. Garnish with the green onion or more fresh basil. Season with ground pepper.

hot tip For nut-free folk, fold in ¼ cup of nutritional yeast instead of using The Parm or use a vegan parmesan product instead!

sweet things

I believe there's always room for dessert, especially (maybe only) when it's homemade. I really love baking for other people. Any occasion means I'm getting in the kitchen and messing up my apron with flour just for the joy of seeing someone else's face light up with surprise and elation. These desserts aren't fussy or pretending to be healthy. There are cakes, cookies, tarts, trifle, cheesecake, and more! This is how I bake. I want it to taste and feel exactly like dessert, not breakfast or a granola bar. So it's baking at its best with all the essentials: flour, sugar, butter, shortening, sprinkles, chocolate, and everything in between.

that dough

MAKES dough for 12 twists,
1 stuffed pizza crust, 16 fritters,
or 12 rolls
PREP TIME 15 minutes

ingredients

- 3 cups all-purpose flour
- 1 tablespoon granulated sugar
- 2 teaspoons quick-rise instant yeast
- 1 teaspoon sea salt
- 1 tablespoon vegetable oil
- 1½ cups warm water (120°F to 130°F)

Did I mention I love bread? Not sure. If you love it as well, this multipurpose quick-rise yeast dough is crucial for when you just need bread! This dough is used in each of the recipes listed below, but I can't wait to see what else you use it for too.

- Cheesy Pesto Bread Twists (page 41)
- Stuffed Crust Pizza (page 139)
- Apple Fritters (page 172)
- Cinnamon Rolls (page 171)

In a large bowl, combine the flour, sugar, yeast, and salt.

Create a well in the middle of the dry ingredients and add the vegetable oil and the warm water.

Fold with a rubber spatula or wooden spoon until the dough comes together to form a sticky ball. Lightly flour a work surface and your hands and knead the dough 10 to 15 times. Use a light sprinkling of extra flour on the dough and your hands when it starts to stick. The final ball of dough should be slightly sticky and soft, but you can still handle it.

For most recipes, you'll let the dough rest on the counter for 10 minutes covered with a tea towel. After the dough has rested, you can wrap it in plastic and refrigerate or freeze it. If proceeding with a recipe, roll out and shape the dough as instructed in the recipe. Once shaped, the dough will require time to proof to double in size.

For recipes like the pizza crust or fritters, you'll let the dough rise to double in size first. After you've kneaded the dough and have the final ball, oil a bowl with 1 teaspoon vegetable oil. Any excess oil on your hands can be patted onto the ball of dough. Place the dough in the bowl and cover with a damp tea towel. Let it double in size in a warm, dark place. This could take 20 minutes to 1 hour, depending on your environment.

If using frozen dough, thaw it in the fridge overnight. Place the thawed dough in an oiled bowl, cover with a tea towel, set aside in a warm, dark place, and let it warm up and proof to double in size before shaping and proceeding with the recipe.

Not all flour is created equal, so if you use a different type of flour, these measurements cannot guarantee the same results. You cannot overhandle this dough. Adding too much extra flour in the kneading process will make the dough tough. Add only light dustings while kneading and handling the dough to prevent it from sticking too much. You can refrigerate or freeze the dough prior to using it. The only exception is for the Apple Fritters, as the dough retains too much moisture, and previously frozen dough will not deep-fry correctly.

cinnamon rolls

MAKES 12 rolls
PREP TIME 25 minutes, plus
up to 1 hour for proofing
COOK TIME 35 minutes

prep ahead

That Dough (page 168)

rolls

That Dough

¼ cup granulated sugar

¼ cup packed brown sugar

1 tablespoon ground cinnamon

3 tablespoons vegan butter,
melted

frosting

1½ cups confectioners' sugar

2 tablespoons vegan butter,
softened to room temperature

1 teaspoon vanilla extract

2 tablespoons nondairy milk

Pinch of seeds from a vanilla
bean pod or vanilla powder
(optional)

What's cozier than smelling fresh cinnamon rolls baking? Probably nothing except cuddling a baby panda, but that's never going to happen! Oooh I wish, I wish. Okay, anyway these soft billowy, gooey rolls layered with cinnamon and sugar are snuggle-worthy nonetheless and will leave you blissed out after just one bite!

For this recipe, the dough is rolled out after it has rested for 10 minutes.

To make the rolls, while the dough is resting, combine the sugars and cinnamon together in a bowl.

Lightly flour a work surface and roll out the dough to a rectangle approximately 18 by 12 inches.

Brush most of the melted butter on the surface of the dough, leaving 1 inch of one long side without butter or filling. Sprinkle the cinnamon-sugar filling evenly on top.

Starting opposite the uncovered edge, roll the dough into a tight log shape. Take a sharp knife and cut 12 rolls, each 1½ inches wide.

Brush the small amount of excess melted butter inside a 9-by-9-inch baking pan or a large cast-iron skillet. Place the rolls in the pan, leaving a bit of space between the rolls and between the rolls and the edges of the pan. Cover the pan with plastic wrap and a tea towel and allow the rolls to rise until double in size in a warm, dark place. This could take 20 minutes to 1 hour depending on your environment. You can leave them overnight and bake in the morning. Do not refrigerate.

When ready to bake, preheat the oven to 350°F. Bake for 30 to 35 minutes until the tops of the rolls are golden brown. Let the rolls cool enough so that you can handle them.

To make the frosting, combine the confectioners' sugar, butter, vanilla extract, nondairy milk, and vanilla seeds in a bowl and mix with a hand mixer or whisk. Spread the frosting over the rolls while still in the pan or spread the frosting on each cinnamon roll individually for serving.

The rolls are best served immediately. Any extras should be stored at room temperature in an airtight container. Leftovers are best served slightly warmed.

apple fritters

MAKES 16 fritters
PREP TIME 30 minutes, plus up
to an hour for proofing
COOK TIME 30 minutes

prep ahead

That Dough (page 168)

fritters

That Dough

2 tablespoons vegan butter

2 cups peeled and diced apples
(½-inch pieces)

¼ cup granulated sugar

½ teaspoon sea salt

1 teaspoon ground cinnamon

4 to 6 cups vegetable oil, for
deep-frying

glaze

2½ cups confectioners' sugar

3 to 4 tablespoons nondairy milk

2 teaspoons vanilla extract

When you're vegan you can't just waltz into a divey doughnut shop and take your pick. Admittedly that's one experience I miss, but I've learned to make every comfort food I yearn for, and apple fritters are definitely at the top of that list! I need you to make these, and to encourage you even more, there are step-by-step photos on page 175 so success is guaranteed. It's a lot of fun making these fritters. You'll feel like a kid mucking with Play-Doh so dive in and get messy!

For this recipe, you'll let the dough rise to double in size before rolling it out and forming the fritters. It's important to make the dough fresh. Do not use dough that's been refrigerated or frozen.

To make the fritters, melt the butter in a pan over medium heat. Add the apples, sugar, salt, and cinnamon. Stir to combine and cook until the mixture is thick and syrupy, 6 to 8 minutes. Turn off the heat and let cool completely.

Place the ball of risen dough on a lightly floured work surface and lightly flour a rolling pin. Roll out the dough to ½ inch thick, to an approximately 10-inch square or 10-inch circle. It doesn't have to be perfect.

Pour the apples and syrup on half of the dough. Fold the other half over the apples and pinch around the edges with your fingers to create a seal. Cut into 1-inch rows in both directions to create a grid of pieces.

Lightly flour the grid and your hands and then smash all of this together to form a loaf shape, pushing any escaping apples into the dough. Take a lightly floured knife or dough cutter and cut the loaf on the diagonal 4 or 5 times and then crosswise again from the other direction.

Now lightly flour this mess and your hands, and grab the dough and apple chunks and form gently into small mounds, smashing each together to seal in the apples as best you can. The mounds should be 2 to 2½ inches in diameter. Place the mounds on 2 floured baking sheets, leaving space between them for rising.

CONTINUED

hot tip When baking or cooking apples, I often gravitate to Granny Smith for tartness but Gala, McIntosh, Honeycrisp, or whatever you have will work just fine.

Cover the baking sheets with plastic wrap and a tea towel and let the mounds rise to double in size in a warm, dark place. This could take 20 minutes and up to 1 hour depending on your environment.

When you are ready to fry the fritters, pour the oil into a deep pot. You need approximately 2 inches of oil. Heat the oil to 360°F on a deep-frying thermometer. Set a wire rack on a baking sheet lined with paper towels, for holding the finished fritters.

While the oil is heating, make the glaze. Combine all the ingredients together in a bowl. Adjust the sugar or nondairy milk if necessary to create a smooth, runny glaze.

It's important to fry the fritters at 360°F to 365°F. If the oil is any cooler, you will get soggy oily fritters; any hotter and they will cook too fast on the outside and harden.

If any apples seem to be falling off just push them into the dough or fold over any excess, but don't handle the fritters too much. Gently place 2 or 3 fritters in the hot oil, adjusting the temperature as needed. Fry for 1½ minutes on the first side, gently flip with a slotted frying spoon, and fry for 1½ minutes on the other side. You may lose a few apples, but you can fish them out with the frying spoon as they float off. Once the fritters are an even golden brown, lift each one with the spoon, letting any excess oil drip back into the pot. Place on a wire rack.

Make sure that the oil is at 360°F before frying more batches.

While the fritters are still warm, dip them into the glaze, allowing the excess to drip off, or gently brush them with the glaze. Place back on the wire rack. I find using a brush helps get an even amount of glaze all over the fritter as well as in any nooks and crannies. The fritters are best served immediately and should be consumed within the first 24 hours.

customizable cake

MAKES one 7- or 8-inch double layer cake or 12 cupcakes
PREP TIME 30 minutes
COOK TIME 15 minutes

chocolate cake

- 1 cup soy milk
- 1 teaspoon apple cider vinegar
- 1 cup plus ⅔ cup all-purpose flour
- 1 teaspoon baking powder
- ½ teaspoon baking soda
- ¼ teaspoon sea salt
- ⅓ cup Dutch-processed cocoa powder
- ¾ cup granulated sugar
- ⅓ cup vegetable oil, or ⅓ cup coconut oil, melted
- 1 teaspoon vanilla extract

vanilla cake

- 1 cup soy milk
- 1 teaspoon apple cider vinegar
- 2 cups all-purpose flour
- 1 teaspoon baking powder
- ½ teaspoon baking soda
- ¼ teaspoon sea salt
- ¾ cup granulated sugar
- ⅓ cup vegetable oil, or ⅓ cup coconut oil, melted
- 1 teaspoon vanilla extract
- Seeds of 1 vanilla bean pod or ¼ teaspoon vanilla powder

apple spice cake

- 1 cup soy milk
- 1 teaspoon apple cider vinegar
- 2 cups all-purpose flour
- 1 teaspoon baking powder
- ½ teaspoon baking soda

These four cake recipes will provide you with the framework and bad-assery for great vegan cakes or cupcakes. I've given you the exact amounts for these flavor variations, but if you want to experiment, make sure you have the same total amount of dry ingredients and wet ingredients and all should go smoothly! Spices, fruits, chocolate chips, or nuts are extra additions that shouldn't mess things up, but no promises. Baking has rules after all, and I certainly don't know all of them. I find using soy milk provides the best results for these particular recipes, but if you can't have soy, substituting another nondairy milk will be fine. You can even substitute apple sauce for the oil!

If you need to double a recipe to make a four-layer cake or two dozen cupcakes, you should still make one batch at a time as opposed to doubling the ingredients in the same bowl. Use 9-inch cake pans so the layers aren't too thick.

Preheat the oven to 350°F.

If making a layer cake, generously oil or butter cake pans and then dust with an even coating of flour to help easily remove cake from the pans. If making cupcakes, insert paper liners in the cups of a standard muffin pan or use a silicon tray placed on a baking sheet if you prefer.

In a bowl, combine the soy milk and apple cider vinegar (include the lemon zest and juice if making the lemon cake). Set aside for 10 minutes.

In a large bowl, sift together the flour, baking powder, baking soda, and salt. If making the chocolate cake, include the cocoa. If making the vanilla cake and using vanilla powder, sift it with the dry ingredients. For the apple spice cake, include the spices. Stir to combine well.

Once the soy milk mixture has thickened, combine it with the sugar, vegetable oil, and vanilla extract. For the apple spice cake, add the molasses and shredded apple. For the vanilla cake, add the vanilla seeds. Stir to combine well.

Pour the liquid ingredients into the dry ingredients and fold with a spatula, scraping the edges a few times as you go until the batter is just

CONTINUED

¼ teaspoon sea salt

1½ teaspoons ground cinnamon

½ teaspoon ground ginger

½ teaspoon ground allspice

¾ cup packed brown sugar

⅓ cup vegetable oil,
or ⅓ cup coconut oil, melted

1 teaspoon vanilla extract

1½ teaspoons unsulphured
molasses

1 cup peeled and shredded apple

¾ cup pecans, finely chopped
(optional)

lemon cake

¾ cup soy milk

1 teaspoon apple cider vinegar

2 teaspoons grated lemon zest
and ¼ cup freshly squeezed
lemon juice

2 cups all-purpose flour

1 teaspoon baking powder

½ teaspoon baking soda

¼ teaspoon sea salt

¾ cup granulated sugar

⅓ cup vegetable oil, or ⅓ cup
coconut oil, melted

1 teaspoon vanilla extract

combined. Do not overmix. Small lumps in the batter are fine, but you shouldn't see pockets of dry ingredients that aren't incorporated.

For the apple spice cake, you can add the pecans to the batter or you can add them later to the frosted cake.

If making a cake, divide the batter between the prepared pans and spread out evenly with a spatula. Slightly shake the pan back and forth to even out the batter. If making cupcakes, divide batter evenly among the prepared muffin cups.

Bake the cakes or cupcakes on the same rack for 14 minutes and check if a toothpick inserted in the center comes out clean at this point. They may be done at 14 minutes or depending on the thickness of the cakes it could take 15 to 18 minutes. Remove the cake pans onto wire racks and let cool for 10 minutes. To remove the cakes, place the wire rack on top of the cake pan and flip it upside down. Let cakes cool completely before frosting and assembling. For cupcakes in paper liners you can lift them out of the muffin cups with a spatula immediately out of the oven and place on wire racks to cool completely before frosting.

buttercream frostings

MAKES icing for 1 double layer
cake or 12 cupcakes
PREP TIME 25 minutes

chocolate buttercream

1 cup vegan butter, cubed and
chilled

½ cup Dutch-processed cocoa
powder

2 teaspoons vanilla extract

2 to 3 tablespoons soy milk

3½ to 4 cups confectioners'
sugar

vanilla buttercream

1 cup vegan butter, cubed and
chilled

2 teaspoons vanilla extract

Pinch of seeds from vanilla bean
pod or pinch of vanilla powder
(optional)

2 tablespoons soy milk

4 cups confectioners' sugar

maple buttercream

1 cup vegan butter, cubed
and chilled

¼ cup maple syrup, or
2 teaspoons maple extract

1 tablespoon soy milk (if
using maple syrup), or 2 to
3 tablespoons soy milk (if using
extract)

4 cups confectioners' sugar

raspberry buttercream

1 cup frozen raspberries, thawed

1 cup vegan butter, cubed
and chilled

2 teaspoons vanilla extract

4 cups confectioners' sugar

**Each of these frostings yields enough to frost the middle and outside
of a double layer cake or a dozen cupcakes. If you need to double the
recipe, make one batch at a time. I find that using a food processor is
the fastest and easiest method. You can also use a hand mixer. The key
to a fluffy frosting is starting with cold butter and whipping it, then
gradually adding the extra ingredients, soy milk, and confectioners'
sugar until the perfect consistency is achieved.**

For the raspberry buttercream, strain the thawed raspberries through
a fine-mesh sieve placed over a bowl, separating the juice from the
seeds. Discard the seeds and reserve approximately 3 tablespoons
raspberry juice. You will use the juice instead of the soy milk called for
in the other buttercreams.

Whip the cold butter in a food processor or with a hand mixer until soft
and smooth.

Add the cocoa and vanilla extract if making the chocolate buttercream;
the vanilla extract and vanilla seeds if making the vanilla buttercream;
the maple syrup if making the maple buttercream; and the vanilla extract
if making the raspberry buttercream. Add 1 tablespoon of the soy milk or
raspberry juice depending on the version you're making, along with 1 cup
of the confectioners' sugar. Mix until smooth. Continue adding the sugar
and soy milk or juice until the buttercream is fluffy, soft, and spreadable.

If not using the buttercream right away, store at room temperature in
an airtight container or cover with plastic wrap. For storage longer
than 24 hours, refrigerate the buttercream; allow it to come to room
temperature before using. You might need to add a small amount of
liquid to smooth out the frosting before spreading.

To frost a double layer cake, place the first cake layer bottom side down
on your serving tray or platter. Using an icing spatula, generously frost
the top surface out to the edges of the cake. The frosting should be
no more than ⅜-inch thick. Place the second cake layer top side down
so you now have a flat surface for the top of the cake. Use remaining
frosting to frost the entire outside of the cake. Decorate as desired. Serve
the same day as baking and frosting for best results. Leftovers can be
stored in the fridge or at room temperature for 2 to 3 days. If refrigerated,
let cake sit at room temperature before consuming to take the chill off.

hot tip If you're making a four-layer cake, you can double the icing recipes. You can also experiment with naturally coloring your frosting using beet powder, blue and green spirulina, matcha powder, turmeric, or other fruit juices and purees.

Tiramisu Trifle

MAKES 8 to 10 servings
PREP TIME 40 minutes, plus chilling mousse overnight and trifle for up to 6 hours
COOK TIME 5 minutes

prep ahead

Vanilla Cake (page 177)

chocolate mousse

2 cups soft tofu (from one 12-oz/350-g brick)

¼ cup raw cacao powder

½ cup granulated sugar

2 teaspoons cornstarch

¼ teaspoon sea salt

whipped cream

3 (13.5 oz/400 ml) cans full-fat coconut milk, refrigerated overnight

1 teaspoon vanilla extract

½ cup confectioners' sugar

cake

2 (7-inch) layers of Vanilla Cake

½ cup hot water

2 tablespoons instant espresso powder

½ cup cold water

¼ cup coffee liqueur

⅓ cup raw cacao nibs or finely chopped dark chocolate

2 teaspoons raw cacao powder

Using a cake recipe, you can make a tasty layered trifle with any kind of fillings you like, but I thought transforming tiramisu into a giant messy pot of chocolate mousse, whipped cream, and coffee liqueur–soaked vanilla cake seemed right up your (well, my) alley. If you want to eat trifle right, ask you're your grandma or auntie for an old-fashioned trifle dish. It's usually 6 to 7 inches wide and 7 inches deep. Then dig into these luscious layers with a big ol' spoon and throw your manners right out the window!

To make the chocolate mousse, combine the ingredients together in a blender until smooth. Pour into a saucepan and heat over medium, whisking constantly for about 5 minutes until the mixture is thick like pudding. Place in a bowl and refrigerate for at least 6 hours, or overnight.

To make the whipped cream, scoop the thick cream from the cans of coconut milk into a large glass bowl, making sure not to get any liquid in the mix. Beat with a hand mixer or in a stand mixer for 4 to 5 minutes until fluffy and smooth. Add the vanilla extract and then add the confectioners' sugar a bit at a time while beating. Once all the sugar is added, beat for another 1 to 2 minutes until fluffy and smooth.

To assemble the cake, trim the edges of the vanilla cake layers so they fit inside the trifle dish.

In a wide dish that can fit the diameter of the cake, combine the hot water with the instant espresso. Add the cold water and coffee liqueur. Stir to combine well. Using a fork or toothpick, prick holes about ¼ inch deep into both sides of each cake. Soak one cake at a time in the espresso mixture for 30 seconds to 1 minute on each side. Use your hands or a spoon to pour some of the espresso mixture over the edges of the cake.

Place one soaked cake in the trifle dish. Top with half of the chilled chocolate mousse and spread out in an even layer. Sprinkle half of the cacao nibs on the mousse. Top with a layer of whipped cream, spread it out to the edges of the dish. Repeat the layers with the remaining soaked cake, mousse, cacao nibs, and whipped cream. Dust the top with cacao powder through a fine-mesh sieve or sifter. Refrigerate for 4 hours. Before serving, allow the trifle to sit at room temperature for at least 20 minutes to take the chill off.

fudgy brownies

MAKES 9 large brownies
PREP TIME 25 minutes
COOK TIME 35 minutes

ingredients

- 2 tablespoons ground flax meal
- 6 tablespoons water
- 1 cup all-purpose flour
- ⅓ cup Dutch-processed cocoa powder
- ¼ teaspoon sea salt
- ½ cup vegan butter
- ⅔ cup vegan chocolate chips
- ¾ cup granulated sugar
- 1 teaspoon vanilla extract
- ½ cup walnuts, coarsely chopped

Brownies come in all shapes, styles, and textures . . . much like humans. But I'd take a pan full of these over social interaction any day. These are a dense, fudgy brownie—crunchy on the outside, soft in the middle. You can make them into squares as pictured or bake them in a mini muffin tin for brownie bites!

Preheat the oven to 350°F. Line a 9-inch square baking pan with parchment paper, allowing the paper to extend beyond opposite sides of the pan, for lifting out the finished brownies, or grease the pan with vegan butter.

In a small bowl, mix together the flax meal and water. Set aside for 10 minutes to thicken.

Meanwhile, place the all-purpose flour in a bowl. Sift the cocoa powder and salt into the flour and stir to combine well.

Melt the vegan butter in a small saucepan over low heat. Remove from the heat, add ⅓ cup of the vegan chocolate chips, and stir until they are completely melted and smooth.

Add the sugar and vanilla extract to the butter mixture and stir or whisk to combine. Add the butter mixture to the dry ingredients along with the flax mixture, another ⅓ cup of the vegan chocolate chips, and the walnuts. Fold together until combined. Scrape the batter into the prepared pan and spread it with a spatula in an even layer out to the edges of the baking pan.

Bake for 30 minutes until a toothpick inserted into the center comes out clean.

Allow the brownies to cool in the pan on a wire rack before lifting out by the edges of parchment paper or cutting into squares.

Store in an airtight container at room temperature and consume within 4 to 5 days.

hot tip You don't have to bake all the cookies at once. Freeze the extra cookie dough for later! Allow the dough to thaw at least halfway before portioning out the cookies and baking. Bake as directed.

oatmeal chocolate chunk cookies

MAKES 4 to 4½ dozen cookies
PREP TIME 30 minutes
COOK TIME 50 minutes

ingredients

1 tablespoon ground flax meal

3 tablespoons water

2 cups all-purpose flour

1 teaspoon baking soda

1 teaspoon baking powder

1 teaspoon ground cinnamon

½ teaspoon sea salt

1 cup vegan butter, at room temperature

1 cup packed brown sugar

1 cup granulated sugar

¼ cup nondairy milk

2 teaspoons vanilla extract

2 cups rolled oats (not quick cooking)

1½ cups vegan chocolate chunks or chocolate chips

Cookies. They're the simplest and most delicious treat. But I do have a problem with cookies masquerading as health food. Why on earth would you compromise what you're really dying for? This is a rich, chewy cookie that is not healthy. It's just the way a good cookie should be . . . I betcha can't eat just one!

Preheat the oven to 350°F. Line 2 baking sheets with parchment paper.

In a small bowl, mix together the flax meal and water. Set aside for 10 minutes to thicken.

In a large bowl, combine the flour, baking soda, baking powder, cinnamon, and salt.

In another bowl, beat together the vegan butter and sugars with a hand mixer or in a stand mixer for 1 to 2 minutes until fluffy. Add the flax mixture, nondairy milk, and vanilla extract to the butter mixture and beat until smooth and fluffy, approximately 1 minute.

Add the wet ingredients to the dry ingredients and fold a few times until half combined. Add the rolled oats and 1 cup of the chocolate chunks. Continue folding until well combined.

Place slightly more than 1 tablespoon batter per cookie on the prepared baking sheets, allowing enough space between the cookies for them to double in size.

I like to use the remaining ½ cup chocolate chunks for the tops of the cookies. Place 1 or 2, or more, pieces on each cookie before baking. This way the chocolate chunks will be visible on top!

Bake one sheet at a time for 10 to 12 minutes. Place the other sheet with prepared cookies in the fridge. You can also place extra cookie dough in the fridge before preparing them for baking the next batches. Watch closely, as you don't want to overbake the cookies, otherwise they'll be crisp rather than chewy. They should be a light golden color and not dark on the bottom or too dark around the edges.

Remove the cookies to wire racks as soon as they come out of the oven, using a spatula. Continue baking the cookies in batches.

Store the cookies between layers of parchment paper in an airtight container at room temperature for up to 4 to 5 days.

baked blueberry cheesecake

MAKES 8 to 10 servings
PREP TIME 30 minutes, plus
at least 4 hours for chilling
cheesecake
COOK TIME 55 minutes

crust

1 cup rolled oats (not quick
cooking)

½ cup packed brown sugar

½ teaspoon sea salt

2 tablespoons vegan butter,
melted

filling

1 cup raw cashews, soaked
in hot water for 20 minutes

1 cup soft tofu

1 cup vegan cream cheese

1 cup granulated sugar

¼ teaspoon grated lemon zest
and ¼ cup freshly squeezed
lemon juice

blueberry topping

2 cups fresh or frozen
blueberries

2 tablespoons freshly squeezed
lemon juice

¼ cup granulated sugar

Making a vegan cheesecake that is indistinguishable from a cheese-cake made from actual cheese is no easy feat. But this is The One, guaranteed. Cherish it! I had all the biggest vegan skeptics I know try it just to be sure, and they didn't even realize it was vegan. You can serve this tangy, creamy cake with any kind of fruit compote you want, but I'll always have a soft spot for blueberries.

Preheat the oven to 350°F.

To make the crust, in a food processor, pulse the rolled oats into a flour. This should be a very fine mixture with no large pieces of oats. Add the brown sugar, salt, and melted butter and pulse until the mixture comes together. It should press together when you pinch it.

Press the mixture in an even layer into the bottom of a 7 or 8-inch springform pan. You can also press it into an 8-inch square baking dish. You can line the dish with parchment paper for easy removal or you can serve the baked cheesecake directly from the dish.

To make the filling, drain and rinse the cashews. Place in a high-powered blender with the remaining ingredients and blend until very smooth.

Pour the filling on top of the crust. Bake for 45 minutes until the edges of the cheesecake are light golden brown. The center might look a bit soft, but it will firm up upon cooling.

Allow the cheesecake to cool completely. Refrigerate it for at least 4 hours or overnight. Only once the cheesecake has chilled completely should you remove the sides of the springform pan. Let the cake sit at room temperature for at least 30 minutes before serving to remove the chill.

To make the topping, combine all the ingredients in a saucepan over medium heat. Simmer for 6 minutes. Let cool before serving over the cheesecake. There is enough blueberry compote to put a good portion on top of the cheesecake and have some extra to add to individual servings.

Store leftover cheesecake in the fridge for up to 7 days.

blackberry crumble bars

MAKES 16 bars
PREP TIME 40 minutes
COOK TIME 40 minutes

crust

- 1½ cups all-purpose flour
- ½ teaspoon sea salt
- ¼ cup granulated sugar
- ¼ cup packed brown sugar
- ½ cup cold vegan butter, cubed

blackberry filling

- 4½ cups fresh blackberries (about 4 pints)
- 2 tablespoons granulated sugar
- 2 tablespoons all-purpose flour
- 1 tablespoon freshly squeezed lemon juice

crumble topping

- ¾ cup rolled oats (not quick cooking)
- ¼ cup packed brown sugar
- ½ teaspoon ground cinnamon
- 3 tablespoons cold vegan butter, cubed

Fruit crumbles are the epitome of fast and rustic baking. Literally, you can't F them up! They're delicious, pretty healthy, and easily customizable. Now, me being me, I kind of fancified the recipe into a delicate crumble bar, which is pretty, but you could very well blow off the bars and use the filling ingredients and topping (minus the crust stuff) for any quick fruit crisp you're craving! Just remember, adding vanilla ice cream is a must for devouring this dessert the right way.

Preheat the oven to 375°F. Line an 8- or 9-inch square baking dish or pan with parchment paper, allowing the paper to extend beyond opposite sides of the pan, for lifting out the finished bars.

To make the crust, in a food processor, combine the flour, salt, and sugars. Add the butter cubes while processing. Combine until the mixture is the texture of fine crumbs. Alternatively, you can combine the flour, salt, and sugars in a bowl and cut in the cold butter with a pastry blender.

Reserve ¾ cup of the crust mixture in another bowl to make the topping. Press the remaining mixture in an even layer into the bottom of the prepared pan. It should be very well pressed and solid. Bake for 12 minutes until the edges are just turning golden brown. Let cool completely.

Meanwhile, make the filling. In a bowl, toss the berries gently by hand with the remaining ingredients until well coated.

To make the topping, combine the reserved ¾ cup crust mixture with the rolled oats, brown sugar, and cinnamon in a bowl. Pinch the cubed butter by hand into the mixture until you have a crumble with small chunks of cold butter. Keep the topping in the fridge until ready to assemble.

Spread the blackberry filling on top of the cooled crust in an even layer with no gaps. If you have any extra blackberries, use them to fill any gaps. Top with the crumble topping in an even layer.

Bake for 25 minutes. For the best results, let cool completely before cutting the bars. Store in the fridge in an airtight container. They're best eaten within 2 days max.

classic apple pie

MAKES 6 to 8 servings
PREP TIME 90 minutes, plus
35 minutes freezing dough and
crust, plus up to 6 hours to cool
before serving.
COOK TIME 70 minutes

filling

2 tablespoons cornstarch

2 tablespoons water

8 cups peeled and thinly sliced
Granny Smith apples

1 tablespoon freshly squeezed
lemon juice

¾ cup packed brown sugar

1 teaspoon ground cinnamon

½ teaspoon ground nutmeg

½ teaspoon sea salt

pastry

2 cups all-purpose flour

1 tablespoon granulated sugar

½ teaspoon sea salt

1 cup cold vegan butter, cubed

½ cup ice-cold water

Baking a pie is like beating the whole video game. You didn't think you could do it, and your hands hurt, but with enough hours of game time it was, like, the biggest achievement of your life. Luckily for you, I've done the legwork and will walk you through every step of the journey with secret tips along the way. Let's up the ante and bake some pie!

To make the filling, combine the cornstarch and water into a slurry in a small bowl and set aside. Toss the sliced apples with the lemon juice in a bowl to prevent them from browning. In a large saucepan over medium heat, combine the sugar, cinnamon, nutmeg, salt, and cornstarch slurry. Toss in the apples and stir until well coated. Heat the mixture, stirring constantly, to cook the apples and create a thick syrup, 8 to 10 minutes. Most of the water should evaporate, and the filling shouldn't be too runny. Allow the filling to cool.

To make the pastry, combine the flour, sugar, and salt in a large bowl. Cut in the cubed butter with a pastry blender until a crumblike texture is formed with pea-size pieces of butter throughout. Create a well in the center of the mixture and pour in the water. Fold the pastry together a few times with a spatula until just mixed but still crumbly. Do not overmix!

Portion half of the pastry on a large piece of plastic wrap. Lift the sides of the plastic over the pastry to bring it together and gently form a ball. Finish wrapping the pastry in the plastic and gently flatten into a thick disk. Do the same with the other half. Refrigerate the pastry for at least 15 minutes before rolling out. You can also leave it up to 24 hours in the fridge, but it may need to sit at room temperature for 5 minutes to soften slightly before rolling out.

Have ready a 9-inch pie pan. Flour the work surface, your hands, and a rolling pin and roll out one portion of the pastry to a round ⅛ to 3/16 inch thick, stopping every couple of rolls to make sure the pastry isn't sticking. Gently lift the pastry and lightly flour again underneath as you go.

The pastry should be at least 3 inches wider than your pie pan all around. Roll the pastry over the floured rolling pin, transfer it to the pie pan, and roll it over the top of the pan. Gently press the pastry into the bottom and

CONTINUED

hot tip Feel free to get fancy with the top crust, by cutting strips and basket weaving or just check instagram for all those fancy cut out pie toppings that I have no patience for.

sides of the pan. Trim any excess, leaving at least a ½-inch overhang for shrinkage when you bake. Prick the bottom and sides of the pastry with a fork. Freeze for 15 minutes.

To help prevent a soggy bottom crust, you will prebake the pastry. Preheat the oven to 425°F. Cut a square of parchment paper larger than the pie pan and place it in the pan so it covers the bottom and sides of the pastry. Fill about halfway to the top edge of the pan with pie weights or any kind of dried bean. Bake for 12 minutes. Remove the parchment paper and pie weights and bake for another 2 to 3 minutes until the edges are just turning golden brown. Remove the crust from the oven, leaving it in the pie pan to cool on a wire rack. Only once the bottom crust is cooled should you roll out the pastry for the top crust. Gently trim any excess from the edge of the prebaked crust with scissors so it meets the edge of the pan.

Flour the work surface, your hands, and the rolling pin and roll out the remaining pastry to a round ⅛ to ³⁄₁₆ inch thick, stopping every couple of rolls to make sure the pastry isn't sticking. Gently lift the pastry and lightly flour underneath as you go.

Fill the prebaked bottom crust with the cooled apple filling in an even layer. Roll the pastry over the rolling pin, transfer it over the filling, and roll over top. Trim any excess overhang where necessary. Fold the pastry over and gently tuck under the bottom edge of the bottom crust all the way around the edge of the pie pan. Use the tines of a fork to press the top into bottom crust as an extra seal. Make a few slits in the center of the top to vent the pie while baking.

Bake for 25 to 30 minutes. At this point, you'll likely notice that the edges are done and golden brown but the top is not. Cut a square of aluminum foil slightly wider than the pie. Cut out a circle in the center that is roughly the circumference of the pie inside the crust edge and discard. Place the foil cover on the pie to protect the edges and continue baking for 10 to 15 minutes. If at any point you need to cover the entire top with foil, do so but allow the pie to bake at least 40 to 45 minutes total.

Remove the pie from the oven and remove the foil. Let it rest in the pie pan on a wire rack for at least 4 to 6 hours before slicing. If you like a real juicy pie, go ahead and serve it after 1 to 2 hours but the slices may not hold together nicely. The pie is even better when left to sit overnight at room temperature. Once the pie has cooled, you can cover it loosely with foil. Refrigerate any leftover pie and warm up leftovers before serving in a 350°F oven with a piece of foil loosely on top.

lemon meringue pie tarts

MAKES 18 tarts
PREP TIME 80 minutes,
plus 4 to 6 hours for chilling
COOK TIME 40 minutes

aqua faba meringue

½ cup liquid from 1 can chickpeas or navy or white kidney beans

¼ teaspoon vanilla extract

¼ teaspoon cream of tartar

6 tablespoons confectioners' sugar

¼ teaspoon xanthan gum

pastry

2 cups all-purpose flour

1 tablespoon granulated sugar

½ teaspoon sea salt

1 cup cold vegan butter, cubed

½ cup ice-cold water

lemon curd filling

¾ cup granulated sugar

1 tablespoon tapioca flour

1 cup soft tofu

1 tablespoon grated lemon zest and ½ cup freshly squeezed lemon juice

½ teaspoon vanilla extract

⅛ teaspoon turmeric (optional, for color)

A classic lemon meringue pie was always one of those things I just relegated to never being able to eat again as a vegan . . . until now! These tarts are extraordinary. The whipped peaks of meringue are made using aqua faba or bean water. Ever heard of it? Well it's one of the most revolutionary plant-based food trends. You can now make meringue from the liquid of cooked beans—it's so insane, I know! The aqua faba meringue contains all the same ingredients you'd use for egg whites, but after a lot of testing I found the only way to get the meringue to really firm up properly was to add a bit of xanthan gum. It's a thickening agent often used as the binder for flours in gluten-free baking. Feel free to replace the lemons with key limes or other citrus fruits for endless variations on this recipe.

To start making the meringue, simmer the bean liquid in a saucepan until reduced by about half, 5 to 6 minutes. Place in a glass bowl and refrigerate until completely chilled.

To make the pastry, combine the flour, sugar, and salt in a large bowl. Cut in the cubed butter with a pastry blender until a crumblike texture is formed with small pea-size pieces of butter throughout. Create a well in the center of the mixture and pour in the water. I fill a cup with ice and water to ensure that the water is very cold. Just make sure you don't get ice cubes in the pastry. Fold the pastry together a few times with a spatula until just mixed but still crumbly. Do not overmix!

Portion half of the pastry on a large piece of plastic wrap. Lift the sides of the plastic over the pastry to bring it together and gently form a ball. Finish wrapping the plastic and gently flatten into a thick disk. Do the same with the other half. Refrigerate the pastry for at least 15 minutes before rolling out. You can also leave it up to 24 hours in the fridge, but it may need to sit at room temperature for 5 minutes to soften slightly before rolling out.

Preheat the oven to 425°F when ready to roll out the crust. Have ready 2 muffin pans or 18 mini foil tart pans. If you don't have 2 muffin pans then bake the crusts in 2 batches, but refrigerate the extra dough and only roll and cut out rounds once the first batch is complete.

CONTINUED

Flour the work surface, your hands, and a rolling pin and roll out one portion of the pastry to ⅛ to ³⁄₁₆ inch thick, stopping every couple of rolls to make sure the pastry isn't sticking. Gently lift the pastry and lightly flour underneath as you go.

Using a 4-inch round cutter, cut out as many circles as you can. Gently press the excess dough together and roll out again to cut out more circles. Place each circle into a muffin cup or tart pan and gently press into the bottom and sides. Pierce the pastry with a fork. Freeze for 15 minutes.

Bake for 18 to 20 minutes until golden brown and flaky. Remove from the oven and place on a wire rack to cool. Once cooled remove the crusts from the pan by gently nudging the edge with a knife or spatula. Place on a baking sheet or large plate. Continue your second batch of crusts if you only have one muffin pan.

Meanwhile, to prepare the filling, combine all the ingredients in a blender and blend until very smooth. Pour into a saucepan and cook over medium heat, whisking constantly, for 5 to 6 minutes until thickened. Let the filling sit for 5 to 10 minutes, so it's not piping hot, but don't let it cool too much or it will gel up and be a little tricky to pour.

Fill the crusts with the filling and refrigerate for at least 4 hours. The filling should be more firm and sticky to touch.

To finish the meringue, beat the chilled bean liquid with a hand mixer or in a stand mixer for 2 to 3 minutes until it looks foamy. Add the vanilla extract and cream of tartar and continue beating until stiff peaks form, 3 to 4 more minutes. Add 1 tablespoon of the confectioners' sugar at a time while beating for another 3 to 4 minutes. Add the xanthan gum last and beat for another 1 to 2 minutes. You'll notice that the meringue will become stiffer and slightly stickier after adding the xanthan gum.

Transfer the meringue to a piping bag with a large star tip or to a large ziplock bag with a small piece of the corner snipped off. Pipe a little swirl of meringue on top of each chilled tart. You can also dollop the meringue however you like on top.

Set the oven to broil and place the baking sheet with the tarts under the broiler once the element is hot. Hold the sheet with an oven mitt and move it around under the broiler to brown the tops as evenly as possible. The tarts will brown almost immediately, and they burn very quickly, so do not leave them unattended. The tarts can be served immediately. Refrigerate leftovers for up to 1 week.

hot tip Whenever you open a can of beans, reserve the liquid, measure it, put it in a jar, label the jar with the amount, and freeze for later use.

This recipe makes enough filling and crust for a whole pie instead of tarts, but if you want to pile the meringue quite high, double the recipe for that.

raspberry funfetti pop tarts

MAKES 8 tarts
PREP TIME 1 hour
COOK TIME 30 to 35 minutes

raspberry filling

2 cups fresh or frozen raspberries

1 cup granulated sugar

2 tablespoons freshly squeezed lemon juice

pastry

2 cups all-purpose flour

1 tablespoon sugar

½ teaspoon salt

1 cup cold vegan butter, cubed

½ cup ice-cold water

raspberry frosting

1 cup confectioners' sugar

1½ tablespoons unsweetened nondairy milk

1 tablespoon sprinkles of choice or shredded coconut, for decorating

If I could travel back in time to my childhood the one thing I would want to change is being allowed to eat convenience breakfast pastries. I just recall all the delectable, mind-altering commercials featuring some kid eating a colorful rectangle of sugar and sprinkles. I remember I also just glared with envy at everyone at school eating them at lunch and recess. My parents wouldn't dare let me eat that crap! And I never ever did, not ever, even as an adult. But this cute homemade version uses the same pastry as the Classic Apple Pie (page 192) and Lemon Meringue Pie Tarts (page 197), and I've got to believe they taste about a million times better than those things that come wrapped in foil. Here's an ode to someone else's youth!

To make the filling, combine all the ingredients together in a large saucepan over medium heat. Bring to a simmer. Once the filling is bubbling, lower the heat and simmer for 10 minutes until slightly thicker like jam.

Strain out the seeds by pouring the mixture through a sieve over another saucepan. Push the mixture back and forth with a spatula to allow a lot of thick jam to strain through the small holes. Simmer for 5 minutes. Turn off the heat and let cool completely at room temperature. The filling will thicken much more as it cools. Reserve 1 teaspoon of the filling to use in the frosting.

To make the pastry, combine the flour, sugar, and salt in a large bowl. Cut in the cubed butter with a pastry blender until a crumblike texture is formed with small pea-size pieces of butter throughout. Create a well in the center of the mixture and pour in the water. Fold the pastry together a few times with a spatula until just mixed but still crumbly. Do not overmix!

Portion half of the pastry on a large piece of plastic wrap. Lift the sides of the plastic over the pastry to bring it together and gently form a ball. Finish wrapping the pastry in the plastic and gently flatten into a thick disk. Do the same with the other half. Refrigerate the pastry for least 15 minutes before rolling out. You can also leave it up to 24 hours in the fridge, but it may need to sit at room temperature for 5 minutes to soften slightly before rolling out.

CONTINUED

Preheat the oven to 425°F. Line 2 baking sheets with parchment paper.

Flour the work surface, your hands, and a rolling pin. Roll out one portion of the pastry ⅛ inch thick and into a rectangle 16 to 17 inches long by 6 to 7 inches wide, stopping every couple of rolls to make sure the pastry isn't sticking. Gently lift the pastry and lightly flour underneath as you go.

Trim the edges slightly so you have an even rectangle shape. Cut the rectangle in half lengthwise and then crosswise into 4 pieces. You will have 8 rectangles approximately 4 inches by 3 to 3½ inches.

Spoon a large tablespoon of the raspberry filling on 4 rectangles. Take a bit of water on a finger and dab the edges of each rectangle. Top with a rectangle of pastry and gently press the edges together from the filling outward to the edges. Use the tines of a fork to seal the edges all around. Place the tarts on 1 baking sheet and freeze for at least 15 minutes. Do the same method with the other portion of pastry and place tarts on another sheet. Bake the frozen tarts first and freeze the second batch for at least 15 minutes.

Bake for 15 to 18 minutes until the tarts are golden brown. Remove the tarts from the baking sheet to a wire rack and let cool completely before frosting.

To make the frosting, combine the reserved 1 teaspoon raspberry filling with the sugar and nondairy milk in a bowl and mix until smooth.

Spoon some of the frosting over each tart and spread across the center. The frosting should drape nicely over the top but still leave the edges of the tart exposed. If the frosting is too thin, add a bit more sugar; if it's too thick to spread, add a bit more nondairy milk. While the frosting is still wet, add the sprinkles or coconut. Allow the tarts to dry completely before storing between layers of parchment paper in a container at room temperature. They are best consumed the same day as baking. A day later, you might want to warm them slightly before eating.

get saucy

Oh yes, I'm a sauce superfan . . . but really, who isn't! Food is nothing without sauces or condiments, and you're more than ready to sauce up your meals with all these ideas. These pages are inevitably going to get splattered and dirty because you'll be referencing them with pretty much every recipe in the book. I advise keeping your faves on hand all the time so you're ready to drizzle, dip, douse, and drown all your cravings!

The nacho cheese

MAKES about 1½ cups
PREP TIME 20 minutes
COOK TIME 10 minutes

ingredients

- 1 cup peeled, cubed white potato (about 1 small potato)
- ½ cup peeled, diced carrot (about 1 carrot)
- ¼ cup vegetable oil
- ¼ cup nondairy milk or water
- 1 tablespoon nutritional yeast
- 1½ teaspoons arrowroot flour
- 1 teaspoon garlic powder
- 1 teaspoon onion powder
- ½ teaspoon sea salt
- 2 teaspoons freshly squeezed lemon juice
- 6 pickled jalapeño slices or to taste, plus 3 tablespoons brine
- 1 tablespoon tomato paste

If The Nacho Cheese were an album, it would be Dr. Dre's *The Chronic*. Not only is it gonna make you feel nostalgic for that ooey gooey sauce you get at the movies or carnivals, but it's also gonna be on repeat in your kitchen! You don't need to feel bad about it either because your new favorite cheese sauce is made from potatoes and carrots. No, that's not a typo . . . it's your mantra.

Bring a pot of water to a boil and cook the potato and carrot until fork-tender, 6 to 8 minutes. Drain the vegetables and immediately place in a high-powdered blender. If you cook the potatoes too long, they will become starchy and your sauce will not be smooth.

Add the remaining ingredients to the blender and combine on high until smooth. Your sauce may be hot enough to serve immediately from the blender. If not, heat it in a saucepan for a few minutes until just bubbling and warm or reheat in a microwave.

When you reheat the sauce, a small amount of nondairy milk or water may be required to get a smooth consistency again.

hot tip This is so good you could make more than you need and freeze it in portions. Can be frozen for up to 1 month. It keeps and reheats very well!

For those nights when you want mac & cheese (page 131) but you're thinking "ain't nobody got time for that," just make a batch of The Nacho Cheese and boil some mac . . . there, done! You could add anything else you want to this easy mac & cheese like broccoli, green peas, sautéed onions, or veggie ground round. Also, if you're nut-free, this is your mac!

the parm

MAKES about ¾ cup
PREP TIME 10 minutes

ingredients

⅔ cup raw cashews, almonds, or pistachios

¼ cup nutritional yeast

1 teaspoon sea salt

Remember in college (maybe even now in adulthood) when you would always have a big shaker of Parmesan in your fridge that never seemed to go bad? We have the perfect replacement that you'll be shaking on everything. And it's made from only three simple ingredients. For a slightly different flavor, you can use salted roasted nuts—just reduce the amount of salt you add afterward.

Combine all the ingredients together in a food processor and process until a fine crumb or meal is formed.

Store in a jar or container in the fridge for up to 3 weeks.

hot tip In a pinch you can make a half batch of The Parm in a coffee grinder. Be sure to clean it thoroughly beforehand!

the tartar sauce

MAKES about 1 cup
PREP TIME 20 minutes

ingredients

1 cup vegan mayonnaise

¼ cup finely chopped dill pickle and 2 teaspoons pickle brine

1 teaspoon garlic powder

1 tablespoon freshly squeezed lemon juice

⅛ teaspoon ground pepper

There's not much to say or divulge about tartar sauce. It's dang good and it's not hiding any secrets because it's basically just dill pickles and mayo. I mean, if you're really lazy just combine those two things and call it a day. But in the hot for food kitchen we keep things fancy AF, so here's the real deal that's slathered on the Filet-O-Tempeh Sandwich (page 100).

Combine all the ingredients in a bowl or jar and refrigerate until using. Consume within 7 days.

the mozza

MAKES about 1¼ cups
PREP TIME 30 minutes
COOK TIME 10 minutes

ingredients

½ cup raw cashews, soaked in hot water for 20 minutes

1 cup unsweetened nondairy milk

1 tablespoon tapioca flour

1 teaspoon nutritional yeast

½ to 1 teaspoon sea salt

½ teaspoon garlic powder

¼ teaspoon onion powder

¼ teaspoon ground white pepper

2 teaspoons freshly squeezed lemon juice

I'm not going to lie. Mozzarella is very hard to re-create in plant-based form, especially in the home kitchen. So truthfully, this is more of a mozza sauce. It doesn't have that über-stringy texture, but the flavor and mind trickery are all there. Expect a thick and gooey version that's creamy, salty, and just tangy enough to peek through many savory dishes. It'll brown up when baked on top of a margherita pizza or a crusty crouton for Gooey French Onion Soup (page 79), or when drizzled on Butternut Squash Cannelloni (page 127). In some of our recipes, you can swap arrowroot or cornstarch for the tapioca, but tapioca creates the best texture for this particular recipe so I wouldn't deviate!

Drain and rinse the cashews. Place in a high-powered blender with the remaining ingredients and combine until very smooth. Start with ½ teaspoon of the salt and adjust to your taste after the sauce is heated in the next step.

Heat the sauce in a small saucepan over medium heat, whisking constantly, until just thickened, 8 to 10 minutes.

You'll use all the mozza in the recipes noted above, but if you have leftovers, refrigerate for up to 1 week. Before using the sauce, you might need to add a little more nondairy milk or water while reheating to smooth it out, or try blending the sauce again.

hot tip You can soak cashews for up to 7 days in the fridge so they're always ready to go! Just be sure to change the water every couple of days. Don't forget, my measurements are always the presoaked amount!

the bbq sauce

MAKES 1¼ cups
PREP TIME 10 minutes
COOK TIME 55 minutes

ingredients

1 cup packed brown sugar

2 cups water

½ cup apple cider vinegar

½ cup tomato paste

2 tablespoons molasses

1 teaspoon mustard powder
or Dijon mustard

1 teaspoon smoked paprika

1 teaspoon sea salt

1 teaspoon garlic powder

1 teaspoon onion powder

½ teaspoon ground pepper

I can certainly empathize with the desire to buy a store-bought BBQ sauce. I do it all the time too . . . because of laziness! But not everything on the shelf is vegan friendly. Be on the lookout for anchovies, regular Worcestershire, honey, and of course "natural flavors" that aren't always plant based either. You may or may not be concerned about that, but in the end it's worth the extra time to DIY. Your recipes will taste more authentic, comforting, and real.

Whisk all the ingredients together in a saucepan.

Bring to a low boil. Reduce the heat and simmer, stirring occasionally, for 40 to 45 minutes until thickened.

Let cool completely before storing in the fridge. Consume within 2 weeks.

The guac sauce

MAKES about 2 cups
PREP TIME 20 minutes

ingredients

2 ripe avocados, pitted and peeled

½ cup full-fat coconut milk

¼ cup freshly squeezed lime juice

1 teaspoon hot sauce

¼ teaspoon garlic powder

¼ teaspoon onion powder

¼ teaspoon sea salt

¼ teaspoon ground pepper

I'm all for a chunky guac, but this sauce is just so smooth and suave you'll want to introduce it to everyone! It is meant to be drizzled and dippable. I've got it smothered on the Spicy Black Bean Taquitos (page 50). You can also put it all over tacos or try it as a dip for fries.

Place all the ingredients in a high-powered blender and blend until very smooth. If your coconut milk has separated in the can, make sure the milk and cream are combined before measuring the milk and adding to the blender.

Refrigerate the sauce and consume within 2 to 3 days.

the sour cream

MAKES about 1 cup
PREP TIME 25 minutes

ingredients

1 cup raw cashews, soaked in hot water for 20 minutes

½ cup unsweetened nondairy milk or water

2 tablespoons freshly squeezed lemon juice

½ teaspoon apple cider vinegar

½ teaspoon onion powder

½ teaspoon garlic powder

¼ teaspoon sea salt

¼ teaspoon ground white pepper

We put this on everything! So don't be a skeptic. This creamy cashew sour cream does the trick to replace sour cream in your plant-based life. It even works well as a base for other sauces, so if you have a little leftover, repurpose it into something new and delicious. Did somebody say cashew-based ranch or creamy French dressing? No, just me hearing voices again?

Drain and rinse the cashews and place in a high-powered blender with the remaining ingredients. Combine on high until very smooth.

Refrigerate for at least 1 hour before serving. The sour cream keeps for up to 7 days in the fridge. I would make and consume this as soon as possible for a fresh taste. This isn't the best recipe to freeze and keep for longer storage.

the maple-mustard dip

MAKES ⅓ cup
PREP TIME 10 minutes

ingredients

¼ cup Dijon mustard or grainy mustard

1 tablespoon yellow mustard

1 tablespoon vegan mayonnaise

1 to 2 tablespoons maple syrup, to taste

This sweet and tangy dip is your substitute for honey mustard, so get dippin' all your faves like vegan chicken fingers, pretzels, onion rings, and the Herb-Loaded Sausage Rolls (page 37), or use it as a sandwich spread. Listen, I'm not going to tell you how to live your life, but just use it when you need a little sweetness to balance things out!

Combine all the ingredients together in a bowl or jar. Refrigerate until serving. Consume within 3 weeks.

the red pepper relish

MAKES 1 cup
PREP TIME 20 minutes
COOK TIME 20 minutes

ingredients

2 cups finely chopped red bell pepper (about 2 peppers)

1 cup finely chopped onion (about 1 onion)

2 tablespoons olive oil

5 to 6 garlic cloves, minced

1 teaspoon sea salt

½ teaspoon red pepper flakes

1 teaspoon Dijon mustard or mustard powder

½ cup sugar

½ cup white wine vinegar

This relish is divine with the Mushroom & Leek Quiche (page 22), but you could also use it in place of a hot sauce to pair with other brunch fare like The Big Brekky Skillet (page 12) or The Best Breakfast Sandwich (page 16). It's even a tasty dip for the Herb-Loaded Sausage Rolls (page 37).

Sauté the bell pepper and onion in the olive oil in a saucepan over medium heat for 3 to 4 minutes until soft and fragrant.

Add the garlic, salt, red pepper flakes, and mustard and sauté, stirring frequently, for about 5 minutes, reducing heat to medium-low so the garlic doesn't burn.

Add the sugar and vinegar, bring to a simmer, and cook, stirring occasionally, for 10 minutes until most of the liquid is absorbed.

Let cool completely before storing in the fridge or serving over warm quiche. Consume within 7 days.

the spicy peanut sauce

MAKES about 1 cup
PREP TIME 10 minutes

ingredients

½ cup water

⅔ cup smooth natural peanut butter

¼ cup low-sodium soy sauce or tamari

2 tablespoons freshly squeezed lime juice

1 tablespoon plus 1 teaspoon sambal oelek (chile paste) or Sriracha

2 teaspoons sugar or maple or agave syrup

Peanut butter, spice, and everything nice! This is the simplest, easiest peanut sauce that you'll want for drowning noodles in over and over again. First peep the Spicy Peanut Noodles (page 121) and then start daydreaming about all the other things you could smother with it.

In a blender, combine all the ingredients together until very smooth or stir together in a jar. If stirring the sauce, you may need to use warm water to smooth out the peanut butter.

Use the sauce immediately or store in the fridge and consume within 7 days. You may need to add more warm water to smooth out the sauce before using in a recipe.

hot tip Switch this sauce up by substituting almond, cashew, or sunflower butter for the peanut butter!

the red sauce & the rosé sauce

MAKES 6 cups
PREP TIME 25 minutes
COOK TIME 1 hour

The red sauce

5 pounds Roma tomatoes
(18 to 20 tomatoes)

2 tablespoons olive oil

1½ cups finely chopped onion
(about 2 onions)

3 garlic cloves, minced

3 tablespoons tomato paste

1 bay leaf

1 teaspoon dried oregano

1 teaspoon sea salt

½ teaspoon ground pepper

½ cup packed fresh basil leaves

The rosé sauce

1 cup raw cashews, soaked in
hot water for 20 minutes

1 cup water

6 cups The Red Sauce

This homemade tomato sauce is so incredibly tasty, and canned tomatoes just don't do it justice. I tried and tested, but the sauce isn't the same. So if you can put in a little nonna-style hustle to make it right, you'll be in spaghetti heaven! The sauce is easy to customize by making it spicy with red pepper flakes or by adding more basil or garlic to your liking. How about bringing a little vegan sausage to the party too? And for some extra richness, add cashew cream for a delectable rosé sauce (instructions follow).

To make the red sauce, cut the tomatoes in half lengthwise and scoop out the seeds and excess watery flesh. This is easiest to do with your fingers by pressing an index finger and middle finger inside each tomato half and running them down the length of the tomato. The seeds should slide out. You don't have to get every single one, just the majority. Cut the tomatoes into a large dice.

Heat the olive oil in a large pot over medium heat and add the onions. Sauté for 2 to 3 minutes until soft and fragrant. Add the garlic, tomato paste, bay leaf, oregano, salt, and pepper. Sauté for 2 minutes.

Add the tomatoes. Tear the basil leaves by hand and add to the pot. Stir to combine and bring to a simmer. Continue to simmer for 15 minutes, uncovered, stirring occasionally.

Remove the bay leaf and set aside. Using an immersion blender, blend the sauce until mostly smooth, getting rid of the large tomato chunks. If you don't have an immersion blender, you can pour the sauce into a regular blender and pulse a few times to get it mostly smooth, then add it back to the pot. Return the bay leaf to the pot and continue to simmer the sauce for 25 to 30 minutes uncovered.

If making the rosé sauce, drain and rinse the cashews. Add to a high-powered blender with the water and blend until very smooth. Stir the cashew cream into the pot of red sauce during the last 10 minutes of simmering. Heat through and serve.

Allow the sauce to cool completely before storing in jars. It can be frozen for up to 3 months.

the hollandaise sauce

MAKES about 1 cup
PREP TIME 15 minutes
COOK TIME 5 minutes

ingredients

½ cup sliced blanched almonds

½ cup unsweetened nondairy milk

2 tablespoons nutritional yeast

½ teaspoon mustard powder

½ teaspoon sea salt

½ teaspoon ground white pepper

¼ teaspoon ground turmeric

2 tablespoons freshly squeezed lemon juice

1 tablespoon white wine vinegar

1 tablespoon vegetable oil

Have you ever Googled how to make real hollandaise? It's rich on rich on rich! Rather than relying on butter and egg yolks for fat and flavor, I make the base with lean, mean almonds. You're definitely serving it with the Tofu Benny (page 20), but it's also a classic pairing with grilled asparagus or other green veggies.

Place all the ingredients in a high-powered blender and blend until very smooth. If you need to thin the sauce, add small amounts of nondairy milk until the desired consistency is achieved.

Heat the sauce over low heat in a saucepan, whisking constantly, before serving. If you overheat the sauce or forget to whisk it constantly, it will thicken and get lumpy. If this occurs, reblend it to smooth it out or add more nondairy milk or water.

When reheating leftovers, you'll definitely need to add a bit more nondairy milk or water to thin out the sauce again. It keeps up to 7 days in the fridge.

the gravy

MAKES about 2 cups
PREP TIME 20 minutes
COOK TIME 10 minutes

ingredients

¼ cup finely minced shallot (about 1 small shallot)

3 garlic cloves, minced

¼ cup vegan butter

1 teaspoon fresh thyme leaves, or ½ teaspoon dried thyme

1 teaspoon fresh rosemary, or ½ teaspoon dried rosemary

½ teaspoon ground nutmeg

½ teaspoon celery salt

⅔ cup roasted tahini

½ cup low-sodium tamari or soy sauce

¼ cup maple syrup

¼ cup low-sodium vegetable stock, or more if needed

2 tablespoons vegan Worcestershire

All the best food is brown. Have you heard that one before? It's true . . . it's a hashtag! This gravy wins best in show for its performance in Waffle-Topped Cottage Pie (page 159) and for smothering the Bangers & Mash (page 161). But feel free to skip the main dishes and drink it directly from the gravy boat when no one is looking. We won't tell!

In a saucepan, sauté the shallot and garlic in the vegan butter for 2 minutes.

Add the thyme, rosemary, nutmeg, and celery salt and sauté for 1 to 2 more minutes.

Stir in the tahini, tamari, maple syrup, ¼ cup stock, and Worcestershire and simmer over low heat for 3 to 4 minutes. Add more stock as necessary to thin out the gravy to your desired consistency.

Allow the gravy to cool completely before storing or freezing. It will keep in the fridge for up to 2 weeks or in the freezer for up to 3 months. When reheating the gravy, add more water or vegetable stock to thin it to your desired consistency. The gravy will not become bland from diluting.

the caesar dressing

MAKES about 2 cups
PREP TIME 30 minutes
COOK TIME 35 minutes

ingredients

- 1 garlic bulb
- 1 tablespoon olive oil
- 2 pinches of sea salt
- ¾ cup raw cashews, soaked in hot water for 20 minutes
- ¾ cup water
- 1 pitted medjool date
- 3½ tablespoons nutritional yeast
- 1 teaspoon sea salt
- 1 teaspoon ground pepper
- 1 teaspoon grated lemon zest and 3 tablespoons lemon juice
- 1 tablespoon apple cider vinegar
- ½ teaspoon Dijon mustard

I've known and loved this dressing longer than I've known and loved John. It has been on the blog since inception and continues to be one of the favorite things I've made. Don't mess with it—it's perfect! If you've never roasted garlic, don't be intimidated. It's easy to do, and the smooth flavor and aroma are what makes this dressing something special.

Preheat the oven to 400°F.

Peel the outer layers from the garlic bulb, leaving a thin layer intact. Cut the bulb in half crosswise to expose the cloves. Coat the cloves with the olive oil and sprinkle each half with a pinch of salt. Place in a small baking pan and roast for 35 minutes until the cloves are browned and soft to touch.

Remove the roasted cloves from the bulb with a fork and place in a high-powered blender.

Drain and rinse the soaked cashews. Place the cashews and the remaining ingredients in the blender and combine on high until very smooth.

The dressing will be slightly warm from the roasted garlic and can be served immediately on the Brussels Sprouts Caesar Salad (page 63). Store in the fridge and consume within 7 days.

hot tip Nut-free folks can substitute crumbled soft tofu for the cashews.

three easy dressings

One very important piece of advice for loving yourself is never buy a premade dip or salad dressing if you can help it! It's a big waste of money, and these products are full of weird ingredients you can't pronounce. Also, it's not so easy to find creamy dressings that are both vegan and delicious, so just make them yourself. This is the holy trinity of dressings and dips: The Classic Ranch, The Thousand Island, and The Creamy Cucumber. They're my saviors when I want to make salad into a comfort food affair and less reminiscent of rabbit food. But they're not just for salad. You'll find them used as sandwich spreads and dips throughout the book. Get in the game and dog-ear this page!

MAKES about 1 cup each
PREP TIME 20 minutes

the classic ranch

ingredients

- 1 cup vegan mayonnaise
- 1 tablespoon finely chopped fresh dill
- 1 tablespoon finely chopped fresh flat-leaf parsley
- 1 tablespoon finely chopped chives
- 2 teaspoons apple cider vinegar
- 1 teaspoon onion powder
- ¼ teaspoon sea salt
- ¼ teaspoon ground pepper

Stir all the ingredients together in a bowl until well combined.

Store in the fridge for up to 10 days.

---

ingredients

- 1 cup vegan mayonnaise
- ¼ cup sweet green relish
- 2 tablespoons ketchup
- 1 tablespoon apple cider vinegar
- 1 tablespoon sambal oelek (chile paste) or hot sauce
- 1 teaspoon onion powder
- 2 tablespoons finely chopped chives
- ¼ teaspoon sea salt
- ¼ teaspoon ground pepper

the thousand island

Stir all the ingredients together in a bowl until well combined.

Store in the fridge for up to 10 days.

hot tip Fresh herbs create a more authentic taste and are preferred, but in a pinch you can use dried. I don't know you, but maybe you like your dip thick and your salad dressing thinned out. Whatever your pleasure just add a tablespoon or two of water or nondairy milk to these 3 recipes once they're made to achieve your desired consistency!

---

ingredients

- ⅓ English cucumber
- 1 cup vegan mayonnaise
- 2 tablespoons freshly squeezed lemon juice
- 2 garlic cloves
- 2 teaspoons apple cider vinegar
- 1 teaspoon finely chopped fresh dill
- ¼ teaspoon sea salt
- ¼ teaspoon ground pepper

the creamy cucumber

Shred the cucumber. Place in a sieve, nut milk bag, or double layer of cheesecloth and squeeze out the excess water.

Place the cucumber and the remaining ingredients in a high-powered blender and blend until very smooth. You can also combine all the ingredients in a jar, but be sure to mince the garlic and chop the shredded cucumber. This will result in a chunkier consistency.

Store in the fridge for up to 10 days. Some of the water from the cucumber may separate. You can shake the dressing to combine again.

the aiolis

Meet The Aiolis! Your friendly neighborhood family you'll want to get to know very well. There's something for everyone here: sundried tomato, roasted garlic, spicy Sriracha, jalapeño-lime, and horseradish-dill. You'll find these used heavily throughout the book, but my hope is that soon enough you'll be such an aioli pro that you'll be able to whip up your own flavorful concoctions in a flash! If you can make your own homemade mayo, do so. It will save you all kinds of dollars! But it's essential to have an immersion or high-powered blender since it's the only way the oil and liquid can emulsify to get the right texture. If you don't have either, you'll have to make the investment in premade vegan mayonnaise, and thankfully there's a ton of products on the market now. What a time to be alive! The mayo and aiolis should be refrigerated and consumed within 2 weeks.

MAKES 1¼ cups
PREP TIME 10 minutes

homemade vegan mayo

ingredients

½ cup unsweetened nondairy milk

½ teaspoon sea salt

2 teaspoons apple cider vinegar

1 teaspoon mustard powder
or Dijon mustard

1 cup vegetable oil (sunflower,
safflower, or canola are best)

If using a blender, place all the ingredients except the oil in a high-powered blender. Start blending on low while you slowly drizzle in the oil, and then increase the speed until the mayo is thick and fluffy.

If using an immersion blender, place all the ingredients in a tall jar or tall plastic container. Submerge the blender, then turn it on and blend until the mayo is thick and fluffy.

MAKES ⅔ cup
PREP TIME 15 minutes

the sundried tomato aioli

ingredients

¼ cup dry-packed sundried
tomatoes

½ cup vegan mayonnaise

2 tablespoons freshly squeezed
lemon juice

¼ teaspoon chili powder

¼ teaspoon mustard powder
or Dijon mustard

¼ teaspoon sea salt

¼ teaspoon ground pepper

Soak the sundried tomatoes in warm water for 10 minutes and then drain. This helps to soften the tomatoes for blending.

Add the sundried tomatoes and remaining ingredients to a high-powered blender and blend until very smooth. Alternatively, use an immersion blender to combine all the ingredients in a tall jar or other container and blend until very smooth.

MAKES about ⅔ cup
PREP TIME 15 minutes

the horseradish-dill aioli

ingredients

⅔ cup vegan mayonnaise

1 tablespoon vegan horseradish

1 tablespoon freshly squeezed
lemon juice

1 tablespoon finely chopped
fresh dill

¼ teaspoon ground pepper

Stir all the ingredients together in a bowl until well combined.

the roasted garlic aioli

ingredients

1 garlic bulb

1 tablespoon olive oil

Sea salt

⅔ cup vegan mayonnaise

1 tablespoon freshly squeezed lemon juice

¼ teaspoon salt

⅛ teaspoon ground pepper

⅛ teaspoon cayenne pepper

½ teaspoon vegan Worcestershire

Preheat the oven to 400°F.

To roast the garlic, peel any excess layers from the bulb, leaving some skin intact. Cut the bulb in half crosswise to expose the cloves. Coat the cloves with the olive oil and sprinkle each half with a pinch of sea salt. Place in a small baking pan and roast for 35 minutes until the cloves are browned and soft to the touch.

Remove the roasted cloves from the bulb with a fork and place in a high-powered blender. Add the remaining ingredients and combine on high until smooth. Alternatively, use an immersion blender to blend the roasted cloves and remaining ingredients in a tall jar or other container until very smooth.

MAKES about ⅔ cup
PREP TIME 15 minutes

the jalapeño-lime aioli

ingredients

1 cup vegan mayonnaise

¼ cup pickled jalapeño slices, drained

Grated zest and juice of 1 lime

¼ teaspoon chili powder

¼ teaspoon sea salt

Place all the ingredients in a high-powered blender and combine on high until smooth. Alternatively, use an immersion blender to combine all the ingredients in a tall jar or other container until very smooth.

MAKES ⅔ cup
PREP TIME 10 minutes

the spicy sriracha aioli

ingredients

⅔ cup vegan mayonnaise

2 tablespoons Sriracha sauce

1 tablespoon freshly squeezed lime juice

Stir all the ingredients together in a bowl until well combined.

acknowledgments

Thank you to YOU . . . for buying this book and using it as a tool for spreading more vegan love. I hope it brings you much inspiration. Share it, love it, and go vegan (if you're not already)!

Thank you the MOST to John. This book wouldn't exist without you. Thank you for always making me laugh and squashing my inner sabotage. I love you, forever.

Thank you to my amazing group of recipe testers: Joseph Rapuano, Bianca Migueles, Laura Takahashi, Zachary Smith, Erin Yantha, Kendra Korinetz, Samantha Antille, Becky Hughes, Veronique Daoust, Kaja Köhnle, Nolwenn Petitbois, and Jon Lubanski.

Thank you to JBC, Nat, Lo, and all the Peace Warriors for helping me through my mental blocks surrounding this cookbook. Your strength and inspiration keep me going!

Thank you to my parents, Richard and Jackie, for always giving me the freedom to make my own choices and letting me follow my dreams.

Thank you to Rick, Ashley, Aimee, Maureen, Morgan, Myia, and all the stars at Kin Community for working so hard and believing in hot for food. This book certainly wouldn't exist had we not connected. Rick, thank you for daring us to give YouTube a real shot. You turned a skeptic into a CEO!

Thank you to Tiffany Astle and the penelopePR team for being great friends and colleagues. You've been so good to me and you helped the hot for food dream become a reality.

Thank you to Sally Ekus. It was divine timing that you emailed me and I'm so grateful you're part of the team. You are a powerhouse! Here's to many more endeavors together!

Thank you to Kelly, Emma, Margaux, Lisa R., Lisa F., and all the amazing women at Ten Speed Press who have helped make this book a reality. You are all incredible! Girl power!

Thank you to Andrea Magyar at Penguin Random House for being authentic, honest, and generous. You helped me realize that making a cookbook was the right thing to do for my heart and soul.

Thank you to Magda Zofia and Vanessa Heins for all the hard work and creativity you devoted to the photography in this cookbook.

Thanks, Snickles, for not helping at all with this book but for always being around when I need a cuddle! Sorry for forcing you into photo shoots . . . forgive me!

—xo Lauren

index

Published in the United States by Ten Speed Press,
an imprint of the Crown Publishing Group, a division of
Penguin Random House LLC, New York.
www.crownpublishing.com
www.tenspeed.com

Ten Speed Press and the Ten Speed Press colophon are registered
trademarks of Penguin Random House LLC.

Library of Congress Cataloging-in-Publication Data
Names: Toyota, Lauren, author.
Title: Hot for food vegan comfort classics : 101 recipes to feed your
   face /by Lauren Toyota.
Description: First edition. | California : Ten Speed Press, [2017] |
   Includes bibliographical references and index.
Identifiers: LCCN 2017033606 (print) | LCCN 2017029179 (ebook)
Subjects: LCSH: Vegan cooking. | Comfort food. | LCGFT: Cookbooks.
Classification: LCC TX837 .T7 2017 (ebook) | LCC TX837 (print) |
   DDC 641.5/36—dc23
LC record available at https://lccn.loc.gov/2017033606

Hardcover ISBN: 978-0-399-58014-7
eBook ISBN: 978-0-399-58015-4

Printed in China

Design by Margaux Keres and Lisa Ferkel

10 9 8 7